THREE WAYS
OF THOUGHT IN
ANCIENT CHINA

Three Ways
of Thought in
Ancient China
by
Arthur Waley

STANFORD UNIVERSITY PRESS
STANFORD, CALIFORNIA

Stanford University Press
Stanford, California
Reprinted by arrangement with George Allen & Unwin Ltd.
All rights reserved

Originally published by George Allen & Unwin Ltd., London, in 1939
First published in the United States by the Macmillan Company in 1940
First published in paperback by Doubleday Anchor Books in 1956;
reissued by Stanford University Press in 1982

Printed in the United States of America
ISBN 0-8047-1169-0
LC 56-5973
Last figure below indicates year of this printing:

04   03   02   01   00

PREFACE

This book consists chiefly of extracts from *Chuang Tzu, Mencius* and *Han Fei Tzu*.[1] These are books by philosophers, and many people assume that to read a book about philosophy, unless one has studied the subject specially, is about as much good as for a layman to pore over a treatise on parasitology.

But there are all kinds of philosophy, and the kind that this book deals with is not at all technical. Chuang Tzu's appeal is to the imagination; he can be understood by anyone who knows how to read poetry. The appeal of *Mencius* is to the moral feelings; the book is meaningless unless we realize that it was written at a time when morality (as opposed to Law) was at stake. Hitherto *Mencius* has not much interested Western readers because it has been studied by itself, without relation to other ways of thought that challenged its ideals. Realism, as expounded by Han Fei Tzu, finds so close a parallel in modern Totalitarianism that the reader, so far from being puzzled by anything remote or unfamiliar, will wonder whether these pretended extracts from a book of the third century B.C. are not in reality cuttings from a current newspaper.

Each of these sources has required a somewhat different treatment. The methods of Chuang Tzu are those of the poet, and in the case of poetry analysis is useless.

[1] The first two were written mainly at the beginning, the last shortly after the middle of the 3rd century B.C.

Attempts have been made to analyse Chuang Tzu's 'system'; but they result in leaving the reader with no idea either of what Taoism is or of what the book is like. This can only be done by full quotation.

In *Chuang Tzu* the contrast between Taoist views and those of other schools is dramatized in imaginary dialogues. I have picked out the dialogues between Hui Tzu, the logician, and Chuang Tzu, as also those between Lao Tzu, the Taoist, and Confucius, which in the original are widely scattered, and put them together. This makes it easier to see what the various disputants stand for. If we do not clearly grasp, for example, that Hui Tzu stands for intellectuality as opposed to imagination, we shall miss the point of many of Chuang Tzu's anecdotes.

The appeal of Mencius, on the other hand, is partly intellectual, and in his case I have combined the methods of analysis and long quotation. Finally, Realism is embodied in short essays which continually overlap one another, and I have found it more convenient to make extracts and arrange them according to subject.

I have been reproached with failing to reproduce the terseness of Chinese idiom. But to reproduce this terseness and at the same time to remain intelligible and preserve a dignified and coherent rhythm is often impossible; on the other hand, there are times when things can be said more shortly in English than in Chinese. A great difficulty lies in the fact that far more words can serve both as nouns and as verbs than is the case in English. Take the following, from the 26th chapter of *Chuang Tzu*: 'A basket-trap is for holding fish; but when one has got the fish, one need think no more about the basket. A foot-trap is for holding hares; but when one has got the hare one need think no more about the trap. Words are for holding ideas; but when one has got the idea, one need think no more about the words. If only I could find someone who has stopped thinking about words (yen) and have him with me to talk (yen) to.'

Here the noun 'words' and the verb 'talk' are both expressed by yen. The whole point of the last sentence is spoilt if I translate the first yen as 'words' and the second yen as 'to talk.' But if I try to bring in 'words' into the translation of the second yen, I can only say 'have a word with,' which implies something quite different, or coin a verb 'to word' ('have him with me to word to') which sounds barbarous and affected. Such are the difficulties of the translator.

I have often written 'Chuang Tzu' (and the same applies to Mencius and Han Fei Tzu) when it would have been more accurate to write '*Chuang Tzu*'; that is to say, to name the book rather than the man. I have done this purely for practical convenience, in order to avoid such awkward phrases as 'In the *Chuang Tzu* it is said . . .', or '*Chuang Tzu* says. . . .'

CONTENTS

CHUANG TZU

EPILOGUE

APPENDIX I

APPENDIX II

APPENDIX III

APPENDIX IV

Chuang
Tzu

PART ONE

THE REALM OF
NOTHING WHATEVER

Stories of Chuang Tzu and Hui Tzu

Hui Tzu said to Chuang Tzu, 'Your teachings are of no practical use.' Chuang Tzu said, 'Only those who already know the value of the useless can be talked to about the useful. This earth we walk upon is of vast extent, yet in order to walk a man uses no more of it than the soles of his two feet will cover. But suppose one cut away the ground round his feet till one reached the Yellow Springs,[1] would his patches of ground still be of any use to him for walking?' Hui Tzu said, 'They would be of no use.' Chuang Tzu said, 'So then the usefulness of the useless is evident.'

Hui Tzu recited to Chuang Tzu the rhyme:

> 'I have got a big tree
> That men call the chü.
> Its trunk is knotted and gnarled,
> And cannot be fitted to plumb-line and ink;
> Its branches are bent and twisted,
> And cannot be fitted to compass or square.
> It stands by the road-side,
> And no carpenter will look at it.'

[1] The world of the dead.

'Your doctrines,' said Hui Tzu, 'are grandiose, but useless, and that is why no one accepts them.' Chuang Tzu said, 'Can it be that you have never seen the pole-cat, how it crouches waiting for the mouse, ready at any moment to leap this way or that, high or low, till one day it lands plump on the spring of a trap and dies in the snare? Again there is the yak, "huge as a cloud that covers the sky." It can maintain this great bulk and yet would be quite incapable of catching a mouse. . . . As for you and the big tree which you are at a loss how to use, why do you not plant it in the realm of Nothing Whatever, in the wilds of the Unpastured Desert, and aimlessly tread the path of Inaction by its side, or vacantly lie dreaming beneath it?

> 'What does not invite the axe
> No creature will harm.
> What cannot be used
> No troubles will befall.'

Hui Tzu said to Chuang Tzu, 'The king of Wei gave me the seed of one of his huge gourds. I planted it, and it bore a gourd so enormous that if I had filled it with water or broth it would have taken several men to lift it, while if I had split it into halves and made ladles out of it they would have been so flat that no liquid would have lain in them. No one could deny that it was magnificently large; but I was unable to find any use for it, and in the end I smashed it up and threw it away.' Chuang Tzu said, 'I have noticed before that you are not very clever at turning large things to account. There was once a family in Sung that possessed a secret drug which had enabled its members for generations past to steep silk floss without getting chapped hands. A stranger hearing of it offered to buy the recipe for a hundred pieces of gold. The head of the family pointed out to his kinsmen that if all the money that the family had made in successive generations through the use of the drug were added together it would not come to more than one or two pieces of gold, and that a hundred pieces would amply repay them for parting with their secret. The stranger carried off the recipe and spoke of it to the king of Wu, whose country was being harried by the battleships of Yüeh. The stranger was put in command of the Wu fleet, and so efficacious was the remedy that despite the bitter cold (for it was a winter's day) the fingers of the Wu sailors never once grew chapped or numbed, and the fleet of Yüeh was entirely destroyed. The land of Yüeh was divided and the stranger rewarded with a fief.

'The sole property of the drug was that it prevented hands from getting chapped. Yet so much depends on the user that, if it had stayed with the man of Sung, it would never have done more than help him to steep floss; while no sooner had it passed into the stranger's possession than it gained him a fief. As for you and your large gourd, why did you not tie it as a buoy at your waist, and, borne up by it on the waters, float to your heart's content amid the streams and inland seas? Instead, you grumble about its gigantic dimensions and say that ladles made from it would hold nothing; the reason being, I fear, that your own thoughts have not learnt to run beyond the commonplace.'

Hui Tzu said to Chuang Tzu, 'Can a man really become passionless?' Chuang Tzu said, 'He can.' Hui Tzu said, 'A man without passions cannot be called a man.' Chuang Tzu said, ' "Tao gave him substance, Heaven gave him form"; how is it possible not to call him a man?' Hui Tzu said, 'I would rather say, Granted that he is still a man, how is it possible for him to be passionless?' Chuang Tzu said, 'You do not understand what I mean when I say "passionless."[1] When I say "passionless" I mean that a man does not let love or hate do damage within, that he falls in with the way in which things happen of themselves, and does not ex-

[1] The '—less' has dropped out of the original.

ploit life.' Hui Tzu said, 'If he does not exploit life, what is the use of his having a body?' Chuang Tzu said:

"Tao gave him substance,
Heaven gave him form;
Let him not by love or hate
Bring this gift to harm.

'Yet here are you,

'Neglecting your soul,
Wearying your spirit.
Propped against a pile of books you drone,
Leaning against your zithern you doze.
Heaven made you sound and whole;
Yet all your song is hard and white.'[1]

When Chuang Tzu's wife died, Hui Tzu came to the house to join in the rites of mourning. To his surprise he found Chuang Tzu sitting with an inverted bowl on his knees, drumming upon it and singing a song.[2] 'After all,' said Hui Tzu, 'she lived with you, brought up your children, grew old along with you. That you should not mourn for her is bad enough; but to let your friends find you drumming and singing—that is going too far!' 'You misjudge me,' said Chuang Tzu. 'When she died, I was in despair, as any man well might be. But soon, pondering on what had happened, I told myself that in death no strange new fate befalls us. In the beginning we lack not life only, but form. Not form only, but spirit. We are blended in the one great featureless indistinguishable mass. Then a time came when the mass evolved spirit, spirit evolved form, form evolved life. And now life in its turn has evolved death. For not nature only but man's being has its seasons, its sequence

[1] That is to say, is concerned with the problems of logic, such as the question whether hardness and whiteness exist separately from an object that is hard and white.
[2] Both his attitude and his occupation were the reverse of what the rites of mourning demand.

of spring and autumn, summer and winter. If some one is tired and has gone to lie down, we do not pursue him with shouting and bawling. She whom I have lost has lain down to sleep for a while in the Great Inner Room. To break in upon her rest with the noise of lamentation would but show that I knew nothing of nature's Sovereign Law. That is why I ceased to mourn.'

Chuang Tzu and Hui Tzu were strolling one day on the bridge over the river Hao. Chuang Tzu said, 'Look how the minnows dart hither and thither where they will. Such is the pleasure that fish enjoy.' Hui Tzu said, 'You are not a fish. How do you know what gives pleasure to fish?' Chuang Tzu said, 'You are not I. How do you know that I do not know what gives pleasure to fish?' Hui Tzu said, 'If because I am not you, I cannot know whether you know, then equally because you are not a fish, you cannot know what gives pleasure to fish. My argument still holds.' Chuang Tzu said, 'Let us go back to where we started. You asked me how I knew what gives pleasure to fish. But you already knew how I knew it when you asked me. You knew that I knew it by standing here on the bridge at Hao.'

When Hui Tzu was minister in Liang, Chuang Tzu decided to pay him a visit. Someone said to Hui Tzu, 'Chuang Tzu is coming and hopes to be made Minister in your place.' This alarmed Hui Tzu and he searched everywhere in Liang for three days and three nights to discover where Chuang Tzu was. Chuang Tzu, however, arrived of his own accord and said, 'In the South there is a bird. It is called yüan-ch'u.[1] Have you heard of it? This yüan-ch'u starts from the southern ocean and flies to the northern ocean. During its whole journey it perches on no tree save the sacred wu-t'ung,[2] eats no fruit save that of the lien,[3] drinks only at the Magic

[1] Identified nowadays with the Argus pheasant, but used by Chuang Tzu in a mythological sense.

[2] The kola-nut tree.

[3] Identified nowadays with the Persian Lilac.

Well. It happened that an owl that had got hold of the rotting carcass of a rat looked up as this bird flew by, and terrified lest the yüan-ch'u should stop and snatch at the succulent morsel, it screamed, "Shoo! Shoo!" And now I am told that you are trying to "Shoo" me off from this precious Ministry of yours.'

Once when Chuang Tzu was walking in a funeral procession, he came upon Hui Tzu's tomb, and turning to those who were with him he said, 'There was once a wall-plasterer who when any plaster fell upon his nose, even a speck no thicker than a fly's wing, used to get the mason who worked with him to slice it off. The mason brandished his adze with such force that there was a sound of rushing wind; but he sliced the plaster clean off, leaving the plasterer's nose completely intact; the plasterer, on his side, standing stock still, without the least change of expression.

'Yüan, prince of Sung, heard of this and sent for the mason, saying to him, "I should very much like to see you attempt this performance." The mason said, "It is true that I used to do it. But I need the right stuff to work upon, and the partner who supplied such material died long ago."

'Since Hui Tzu died I, too, have had no proper stuff to work upon, have had no one with whom I can really talk.'

It was not always by dialogue that Chuang Tzu warred with the logicians. Another of his weapons was parody. A favourite method of the argumentative school of philosophy was to take an imaginary case: 'take the case of a man who . . . ,' they constantly say to illustrate their argument.

'Take the case of some words,' Chuang Tzu says, parodying the logicians, 'I do not know which of them are in any way connected with reality or which are not at all connected with reality. If some that are so connected and some that are not so connected are connected with one another, then as regards truth or falsehood the former cease to be in any way different from the latter. However, just as an experiment, I will now say them: 'If there was a beginning, there must have been a time before the beginning began, and if there was a time before the beginning began, there must have been a time before the time before the beginning began. If there is being, there must also be not-being. If there was a time before there began to be any not-being, there must also have been a time before the time before there began to be any not-being. But here am I, talking about being and not-being and still do not know whether it is being that exists and not-being that does not exist, or being that does not exist and not-being that really exists! I have spoken, and do not know whether I have said something that means anything or said nothing that has any meaning at all.

'Nothing under Heaven is larger than a strand of gossamer, nothing smaller than Mt. T'ai. No one lives longer than the child that dies in its swaddling-clothes, no one dies sooner than P'êng Tsu.[1] Heaven and earth were born when I was born; the ten thousand things and I among them are but one thing.' All this the sophists have proved. But if there were indeed only one thing, there would be no language with which to say so. And in order that anyone should state this, there must be more language in which it can be stated. Thus their one thing together with their talk about the one thing makes two things. And their one thing together with their talk and my statement about it makes three things. And so it goes on, to a point where the cleverest mathematician could no longer keep count, much less an ordinary man. Starting with not-being and going on to being, one soon gets to three. What then would happen if one started with being and went on to being?'

[1] The Chinese Methusaleh.

And again.

Suppose I am arguing with you, and you get the better
of me. Does the fact that I am not a match for you
mean that you are really right and I am really wrong? Or
if I get the better of you, does the fact that you are not
a match for me mean that I am really right and you
really wrong? Must one of us necessarily be right and
the other wrong, or may we not both be right or both be
wrong? But even if I and you cannot come to an understanding, someone else will surely be a candle to our
darkness? Whom then shall we call in as arbitrator in
our dispute? If it is someone who agrees with you, the
fact that he agrees with you makes him useless as an
arbitrator. If it is someone who agrees with me, the fact
that he agrees with me makes him useless as an arbitrator. If it is someone who agrees with neither of us, the
fact that he agrees with neither of us makes him useless
as an arbitrator. If it is someone who agrees with both of
us, the fact that he agrees with us both makes him useless as an arbitrator. So then I and you and he can never
reach an understanding. Are we then to go on piling
arbitrator upon arbitrator in the hope that someone will
eventually settle the matter? This would lead to the
dilemma of the Reformation and the Sage.[1]

If we are not thus to wait in vain, what can we do
but smooth out our differences with the Heavenly
Pounder, entrust them to the care of eternity, and thus
live out our days in peace? What is meant by smoothing
out our differences with the Heavenly Pounder? It means
the smoothing away of 'is' and 'is not,' of 'so' and 'not
so.' If what 'is' really 'is,' if what 'is not' really 'is not,'
then what 'is' would be different from what 'is not,'
and there would be no room for argument. If what 'is
so' really 'is so,' it would be different from what 'is not

[1] This disordered world can only be reformed by a Sage
(shêng); but so long as the world is disordered, no Sage
can appear.

so,' and there would be no room for argument. Forget
. . . forget. . . . Both were split off from the infinite,
and may be fitted back again on to the infinite.

To be worked up about the difference between
things that are really the same is called Three in the
morning.

What is meant by Three in the morning? In Sung[1]
there was a keeper of monkeys. Bad times came and he
was obliged to tell them that he must reduce their ration
of nuts. 'It will be three in the morning and four in the
evening,' he said. The monkeys were furious. 'Very well
then,' he said, 'you shall have four in the morning and
three in the evening.' The monkeys accepted with delight.

The last chapter of *Chuang Tzu* consists of an
account of the various philosophers and their schools.
The final section is devoted to Hui Tzu. The text is
very corrupt, particularly in the passages which refer
to the paradoxes defended by Hui Tzu and his
followers.[2] I will translate the more intelligible parts:

Hui Tzu mastered many disciplines. When he travelled his books filled five wagons. His doctrines were
contradictory and devious and his explanations of them
were not successful. . . . He gave to the infinitely large
which can have nothing beyond it the name Great
Unity, and to the infinitely small which can have
nothing inside it the name Small Unity. . . . He under-

[1] I have added a few details from the better version of
the story in *Lieh Tzu*, II, q.

[2] For an attempt to restore these passages and extract a
meaning out of them, see Fung Yu-lan, *History of
Chinese Philosophy* (translated by D. Bodde), p. 197
seq.

took to prove that the sky is lower than the earth, that mountains are no higher than marsh lands, that the sun at noon is on the horizon, that what lives is at the same time dead . . . that one can start for Yüeh today and arrive there yesterday. . . . He maintained that all creatures ought to be held in equal affection and that Heaven and Earth were of one substance.

Owing to his defence of these views he became a general object of curiosity and caused a great stir among the rhetoricians, who vied with one another in their delight at his performances. . . .

Day after day he pitted his cleverness against the ready wit of his opponents and performed prodigies of dispute with all the most accomplished debaters under Heaven. . . . Weak in Inner Power, concentrated upon exterior things—his way was a narrow one indeed! Contrasted with the great Tao of Heaven and Earth, Hui Tzu's capacities seem of no greater consequence than the strivings of a single fly or gnat. . . .

He could find no contentment in what was in him, but dissipated his strength first on one outside thing, then on another; to be known in the end only as a clever debater. Alas, he wasted his great natural gifts in a profusion of effort, and got nothing in return. He pursued thing after thing, and found no end to his quest. He was like one trying to stop the echo by shouting at it, or like substance trying to outrun shadow. Sad indeed!

Stories of Lao Tzu and Confucius

Just as the conflict between mysticism and logic is dramatized in the dialogues between Chuang Tzu and Hui Tzu, so too is the conflict between the mystics and the humanitarian moralists dramatized in a long series of dialogues. This time it is Lao Tzu, the legendary founder of Taoism, who speaks on one side; and no less a person than Confucius on the other.

When Confucius was in the West, he wanted to present copies of his works to the Royal House of Chou. A disciple advised him, saying, 'I have heard that there is a former Royal Librarian called Lao Tzu, who now lives in retirement at his home. If you, Sir, want to get your books accepted at the Library, you had bettter see if you can secure his recommendation.' 'A good idea,' said Confucius, and went to see Lao Tzu, who received the project very coldly. Whereupon Confucius unrolled a dozen treatises and began to expound them. Lao Tzu interrupted him, saying, 'This is going to take too long. Tell me the gist of the matter.' 'The gist of the matter,' said Confucius, 'is goodness and duty.' 'Would you pray tell me,' said Lao Tzu, 'are these qualities natural to man?' 'Indeed these are,' said Confucius. 'We have a saying that gentlemen

'Without goodness cannot thrive,
Without duty cannot live.

Goodness and duty are indeed natural to man. What else should they be?' 'And what pray, do you mean by goodness and duty?'

'To have a heart without guile,
To love all men without partiality,

that,' said Confucius, 'is the true state of goodness and duty.'

'Hum,' said Lao Tzu, 'the second saying sounds to me dangerous. To speak of "loving all men" is a foolish exaggeration, and to make up one's mind to be impartial is in itself a kind of partiality. If you indeed want the men of the world not to lose the qualities that are natural to them, you had best study how it is that Heaven and Earth maintain their eternal course, that the sun and moon maintain their light, the stars their serried ranks, the birds and beasts their flocks, the trees and shrubs their station. Thus you too shall learn to guide your steps by Inward Power, to follow the course that the Way of Nature sets; and soon you will reach a goal where you will no longer need to go round laboriously advertising goodness and duty, like the town-crier with his drum, seeking for news of a lost child. No, Sir! What you are doing is to disjoint men's natures!'

Confucius visited Lao Tzu and began talking about goodness and duty. 'Chaff from the winnower's fan,' said Lao Tzu, 'can so blear our eyes that we do not know if we are looking north, south, east, or west; at heaven or at the earth. One gnat or mosquito can be more than enough to keep us awake a whole night. All this talk of goodness and duty, these perpetual pin-pricks, unnerve and irritate the hearer; nothing, indeed, could be more destructive of his inner tranquillity. . . . The swan does not need a daily bath in order to remain white; the crow does not need a daily inking in order to remain black. . . . When the pool dries up, fish makes room for fish upon the dry land, they moisten one another with damp breath, spray one another with foam from their jaws. But how much better are they off when they can forget one another, in the freedom of river or lake!'

Confucius said to Lao Tzu, 'I have edited the Songs, the Book of History, the Rites, the Canon of Music, the Book of Changes, the Chronicle of Springs and Autumns—six scriptures in all—and I think I may say that I have thoroughly mastered their import. Armed with this knowledge I have faced seventy-two rulers, expounding the Way of former kings, the achievements of Chou and Shao;[1] but there was not one ruler who made the slightest use of my teaching. It seems that

[1] The dukes of Chou and Shao, sons of the founder of the Chou dynasty; traditional date, 12th century B.C.

either my hearers must have been singularly hard to convince, or the Way of the former kings is exceedingly difficult to understand.'

'It is a lucky thing,' said Lao Tzu, 'that you did not meet with a prince anxious to reform the world. Those six scriptures are the dim footprints of ancient kings. They tell us nothing of the force that guided their steps. All your lectures are concerned with things that are no better than footprints in the dust. Footprints are made by shoes; but they are far from being shoes.'

There is another story in *Chuang Tzu* which illustrates his attitude towards book-learning:

Duke Huan of Ch'i was reading a book at the upper end of the hall; the wheelwright was making a wheel at the lower end. Putting aside his mallet and chisel, he called to the Duke and asked him what book he was reading. 'One that records the words of the Sages,' answered the Duke. 'Are those Sages alive?' asked the wheelwright. 'Oh, no,' said the Duke, 'they are dead.' 'In that case,' said the wheelwright, 'what you are reading can be nothing but the lees and scum of bygone men.' 'How dare you, a wheelwright, find fault with the book I am reading? If you can explain your statement, I will let it pass. If not, you shall die.' 'Speaking as a wheelwright,' he replied, 'I look at the matter in this way; when I am making a wheel, if my stroke is too slow, then it bites deep[1] but is not steady; if my stroke is too fast, then it is steady, but does not go deep. The right pace, neither slow nor fast, cannot get into the hand unless it comes from the heart. It is a thing that cannot be put into words; there is an art in it that I cannot explain to my son. That is why it is impossible for me to let him take over my work, and here I am at the age of seventy, still making wheels. In my opinion it

[1] In this whole passage I have used the text as given in *Huai-nan Tzu*, XII.

must have been the same with the men of old. All that
was worth handing on, died with them; the rest, they
put into their books. That is why I said that what you
were reading was the lees and scum of bygone men.'

One day when Confucius went to see Lao Tzu, it was
evident that Lao Tzu had been washing his hair, which
was spread out to dry. Lao Tzu himself sat so utterly
motionless that one could not believe a human being
was there at all. Confucius withdrew, and waited. After
a while he presented himself again, and said, 'Did it
really happen or was it an enchantment? A little while
ago this body, these limbs of yours seemed stark and
lifeless as a withered tree. It was as though you had
severed yourself from men and things, and existed in
utter isolation.' 'Yes,' said Lao Tzu, 'I had voyaged to
the World's Beginning.' 'Tell me what that means,' said
Confucius. 'The mind is darkened by what it learns
there and cannot understand; the lips are folded, and
cannot speak. But I will try to embody for you some
semblance of what I saw. I saw Yin, the Female Energy,
in its motionles grandeur; I saw Yang, the Male Energy,
rampant in its fiery vigour. The motionless grandeur
came up out of the earth; the fiery vigour burst out
from heaven. The two penetrated one another, were
inextricably blended and from their union the things of
the world were born.'

Whether or not the passages in Lao Tzu where frugality is extolled are to be taken literally or figuratively, it is certain that the Lao Tzu of popular legend
figures as economical in the most literal and concrete
sense, and it is in this connection that we are introduced to the only recorded member of his family,
that somewhat mysterious figure, Lao Tzu's sister.

Shih-ch'êng Ch'i visited Lao Tzu and said to him,
'Hearing that you were a holy man I was so anxious to
visit you that I was not deterred by the long road that

lay before me. Night and day I pressed onward through the hundred stages of the journey till my heels were blistered; yet I never dared to rest. But now that I have come I find that you are not a holy man. I saw you take some remains of a salad that had been thrown on to the rubbish-heap and give them to your sister to eat. This was inhumane. I saw you put aside for another time food uncooked and cooked that had not been eaten up at your meal today. This was ill-bred.'

Lao Tzu remained completely unmoved and did not reply. Next day Shih-ch'êng Ch'i visited Lao Tzu again, and said to him, 'Yesterday I found fault with you. Today I see that I should not have done so. How was it that you remained completely indifferent and did not even reply?' 'The titles of clever, wise, divine, holy,' said Lao Tzu, 'are things that I have long ago cast aside, as a snake sheds its skin. Yesterday if you had called me an ox, I should have accepted the name of ox; if you had called me a horse, I should have accepted the name of horse. Wherever there is a substance and men give it a name, it would do well to accept that name; for it will in any case be subject to the prejudice that attaches to the name. If I submitted, it was not because I submitted to you, but because my every act is to submit.'

In the following story a certain Yang Tzu-chü plays the part of the self-important Sage, elsewhere assigned to Confucius.

Yang Tzu-chü was going southwards, to P'ei; Lao Tzu was travelling to the west, towards Ch'in. Arriving at the frontier of Ch'in, at a place called Liang, he met Lao Tzu.[1] Lao Tzu, in the middle of the road, raised his eyes to heaven and sighed saying, 'There was a time when, from what I heard, it seemed as though something might be made of you. But I see now that there is

[1] It would be a mistake to fly to the map. The writer of this passage certainly had none in front of him.

no hope.' Yang Tzu-chü did not reply; but when they reached the inn, he brought water to rinse the hands and mouth, produced towel and comb, left his shoes outside the door and creeping on his knees appeared before Lao Tzu saying,[1] 'This afternoon you raised your eyes to heaven and sighed saying, "There was a time when it seemed as though something might be made of you. But I see now that there is no hope." I longed to ask you to explain what you meant. But as you were in a hurry, I did not venture to do so. Now that you are at leisure, I should like to ask what you consider to be wrong with me.' Lao Tzu said:

> 'With such self-importance, such consequential airs
> Who could live under the same roof?
> What is blankest white looks blurred,
> The "power" (tê) that is most sufficing looks inadequate.'

A troubled look came over Yang Tzu-chü's countenance. 'I will take this to heart,' he said.

When he first arrived at the inn, everyone in the place turned out to meet him. The keeper of the inn brought him a mat, the innkeeper's wife brought him towel and comb. His fellow-guests made way for him; the kitchen-men retreated from the stove. But when the time came for him to depart, so changed was he by Lao Tzu's lesson that people were already pushing him off his own mat.

The Ancients

When Confucius was about to travel westward to the land of Wei, his disciple Yen Hui asked the music-master

[1] The passage is defective in *Chuang Tzu*, and I have used *Lieh Tzu*, II. 14.

Chin, 'What do you think about the Master's journey?'
'I am sorry to say,' replied Chin, 'that your Master will
certainly fail.' 'Why do you think so?' said Yen Hui.
'Before the straw dogs are presented at the altar,' said
the music-master Chin, 'they are kept in boxes . . . under
an awning of brocade; so sacred are they that the Dead
One[1] and Reciter must first purify themselves by fasting
and abstinence before they can handle them. But once
they have been presented, a temple servant destroys them,
crushing head and spine with his foot, the scavengers
remove them and burn them; they are done with for
ever. For it is known that if after the dedication they were
put back again in their boxes . . . under the awning of
brocade, anyone who lodged and slept in their presence
so far from getting the dream he wanted, would be
continually beset by nightmares.

'The "former kings" that your Master applauds, what
are they but straw dogs that have had their day? Yet he
takes his disciples to lodge and sleep in their presence.
Small wonder that the tree under which he taught in
Sung was cut down, that his footprints were erased in
Wei, that he failed alike in Chou and Shang.[2] What
were all these afflictions but the bad dreams that haunt
those who meddle with the dead and done? . . . If, because a boat has taken well to the water, one tries to
travel in it by land, one may push till the end of one's
life and get no further than a couple of yards. Our time
and that of the Former Kings are as different as land from
water; the Empire of Chou over which they ruled and
this land of Lu are as different as boat from chariot. Your
Master tries to treat the Lu of today as though it were
the Chou of long ago. This is like pushing a boat over
dry land. Not only is he labouring in vain; he is bound
to bring himself to disaster. . . . Take a monkey and dress
it up in the robes of our ancestor duke Tan. It would
certainly not be happy till it had bitten and clawed every

[1] The boy who impersonates the dead ancestor.
[2] I.e. Sung.

scrap of clothing from its back; and surely the days of old are no less different from today than a monkey is different from duke Tan?

'Once when Hsi Shih, the most beautiful of women, was frowning and beating her breast, an ugly woman saw her and thought, "Now I have found out how to become beautiful!" So she went home to her village and did nothing but frown and beat her breast. When the rich men of the village saw her, they bolted themselves into their houses and dared not come out; when the poor people of the village saw her they took wife and child by the hand and ran at top speed. This woman had seen that someone frowning was beautiful and thought that she had only to frown in order to become beautiful.

'No, I am sorry to say I do not think your Master will be a success.'

The Brigand and the Sage

Confucius was on friendly terms with the sage Liu-hsia Hui. Liu-hsia Hui had a younger brother who was known as the Brigand Chih. This brigand and the nine thousand followers who formed his band swept through the country, pillaging and despoiling every kingdom under Heaven, burrowing their way into houses, wrenching doors, driving off men's cattle and horses, seizing their wives and daughters. In his greed for gain the brigand forgot all ties of kinship, paid no heed to father, mother, or brothers young and old, and made no offerings to his ancestors. Whenever he approached a town, if it was a big place the people manned the city-walls and if it was a small place they ensconced themselves behind their barrows. The whole countryside groaned under the affliction.

Confucius said to Liu-hsia Hui, 'A father who is worthy of the name ought to be able to correct his son; an elder brother who is worthy of the name ought to be capable of instructing his younger brother. If it is not the duty of fathers to call their sons to order and of elder brothers to instruct their younger brothers, the whole importance that we attach to those relationships at once disappears. But here are you, admittedly one of the most gifted men of your generation; yet your younger brother is known as "the brigand Chih," has become a curse to the whole land, and you have failed to teach him better ways. Forgive me for saying so, but I blush on your behalf. I hope you will not take it amiss if I go in your stead and have a talk with him.' 'You say,' replied Liu-hsia Hui, 'that a father ought to be able to correct his son, that an elder brother ought to be capable of instructing his younger brother. But suppose the son does not listen to his father, suppose the younger brother does not accept the elder brother's advice? In the present case even such eloquence as yours cannot possibly have the slightest effect. My brother Chih is a remarkable man. His passions, once aroused, leap like a fountain; his calculations are swift as a whirlwind. Not only is he strong enough to defy every foe; he is also clever enough to justify every crime. Humour him, and he is friendly; thwart him and he flies into a rage. On such occasions the language he uses is far from flattering; I certainly advise you not to go near him.'

Confucius did not listen to this warning, but taking his disciple Yen Hui to drive the carriage and putting Tzu-kung on his right, he set off to visit the brigand Chih. The brigand and his men happened at the time to be resting on the southern slopes of the T'ai-shan, and were enjoying a supper of minced human liver. Confucius got down from his carriage and went towards the camp. Being confronted by a sentinel he said to him: 'Pray inform the General that K'ung Ch'iu[1] of the

[1] I.e. Confucius.

land of Lu, having heard of his Excellency as a champion of morality, has come to pay his respects.' And so saying he prostrated himself twice before the sentinel with solemnity. When the message was brought, the brigand Chih fell into a mighty rage. His eyes blazed like fiery comets, his hair stood on end so that his hat was lifted off his head. 'Why this is that crafty fraud from Lu, K'ung Ch'iu, isn't it? Tell him from me that it is mere talk for the sake of talking—all this random chatter about his heroes king Wên and king Wu. Dresses up in a forked hat that looks as though a tree had taken root on his head, puts the whole flank of a dead ox round his belly and then chatters unceasingly, heaping nonsense upon nonsense; eats what others have grown, wears what others have woven, wags his lips and drums his tongue, deluding all the rulers under heaven with his own private notions of right and wrong and preventing the scholars who come to him from every corner of the land from using the powers that are in them! Pretends to be interested only in filial piety and brotherly obedience, but spends his time currying favour with landed lords, with the rich and great! Tell the fellow that he is a scoundrel for whom no punishment would be too great, and that if he does not clear out of here at once, we shall add his liver to our morning stew.'

The message was delivered; but Confucius again asked for an interview. 'Being fortunate enough to know your brother Liu-hsia Hui,' he said, 'I desire to look at your feet beneath the curtain.'[1]

The sentinel brought in the message, and this time the brigand Chih said, 'Bring him in!' Confucius advanced at a brisk trot,[2] carefully avoided treading upon the brigand's mat, ran backwards a few steps, and prostrated himself twice.

The brigand was evidently in a great rage. His feet

[1] I.e. to be allowed even the most cursory contact with you.

[2] A sign of respect.

were planted wide apart, he was fingering the blade of
his sword, his eyes glared, and finally with a voice like
that of a suckling tigress he roared out, 'Come here,
Ch'iu! And remember, if what you say is acceptable to
me, you live; if it is not acceptable, you die!'

'I have heard,' said Confucius, 'that there are among
the men of the world three kinds of personal power
(tê). To grow to a stature so commanding, to possess
beauty and grace so incomparable as to delight the eyes
of all men, high or humble, young or old—this is the
highest sort of power. To have a knowledge that em-
braces heaven above and earth below, to have abilities
that can cope with every possible situation—this is the
second and lower sort of power. To be bold, ruthless,
undeterred by any hazard, a gatherer of multitudes and
a causer of wars—this is the third and lowest kind of
personal power. To possess any one of these three is sufficient to set a man with his face turned to the south
and to give him the title of Lonely One.[1] You, my
General, possess all three. Your stature is 8 feet 2
inches,[2] your countenance is dazzling, your lips are as
though smeared with cinnabar, your teeth are like a row
of shells, your voice booms like the tone-note of the
scale. And yet for all this, men call you the Brigand
Chih! I confess I am ashamed on your behalf and cannot reconcile myself to this. But if you will listen to me,
I will go as your ambassador to the courts of Wu and
Yüeh in the south, of Ch'i and Lu in the north, of Sung
and Wei in the east, of Chin and Ch'u in the west,[3]
and arrange that a great walled city shall be built for
you, several hundred leagues in circumference, with

[1] When the ruler faces his subjects, he alone faces to the
south; his subjects face north. He is the Lonely One
(Orphan) because his position is unique and perhaps
also because the father whom he has succeeded is necessarily dead.

[2] About 5 feet 8 inches in our measurement.

[3] The geography of this promise is somewhat confused.

quarters for many hundred thousand inhabitants. You shall be raised to the dignity of a feudal prince, and under your sway the whole world shall begin anew. You will lay down your arms, disband your followers, gather about you brothers old and young, and see to it that they lack nothing; and make due offering to your ancestors. You will thus be behaving like a Sage and Hero and at the same time giving to the world that for which it ardently longs.'

'Listen here,' cried the brigand Chih, in a great rage. 'It is only the ignorant low rabble who allow themselves to be beguiled by promises of gain or scolded into altering their ways. My tall stature and my good looks which delight the eyes of all who see me—these are advantages that I inherited from my parents. I am the person most likely to be aware of them and stand in no need of your approbation. Moreover, it is commonly said that those who are prone to praise men to their faces, are quick to speak ill of them behind their backs.

'And now as to your talk of a great city and a multitude of inhabitants—this is merely an attempt to dazzle me by promises of gain, and is treating me as though I were a common, witless peasant. And even if such success were attainable, how long would it be secured? The biggest city cannot be larger than the world. The Emperors Yao and Shun[1] possessed the whole world, yet their sons and grandsons had not so much as a pin-point of land. T'ang of the Yin dynasty, Wu of the Chou dynasty rose to be Sons of Heaven; but their posterity is extinct. Was not this just because what they sought and won was far too large a prize? . . . Neither Yao nor Shun could set a son upon the throne; both made way for subjects. T'ang of Yin banished his sovereign; king Wu of Chou slew Chieh[2] of Yin. And from that day onward the strong have crushed the weak, the many have maltreated the few; nor since the time of T'ang and

[1] Legendary 'good kings.'
[2] Semi-legendary tyrant.

Wu has there been a single ruler who was not as great a ruffian as they. Yet here come you, earnestly applying yourself to the Way of king Wên and king Wu and using every sophistry under heaven in order to inculcate it upon generations to come. You dress up in a wide cloak and belt of clipped bull's hide, and by your cant and humbug delude the princes of the world into giving you the wealth and honours that are your only real ambition. There can be no greater brigand than you, and instead of talking so much about the brigand Chih, I wonder people do not call you the brigand Confucius!
. . .

'There is no need for you to say a word more. If you could tell me about the affairs of ghosts or hobgoblins, it would be another matter. About them I admit I know nothing at all. But concerning human affairs nothing you say can possibly carry me any further. I shall have heard it all before. I, on the other hand, intend to tell you something about man and his natural desires. He has an eye that longs for beauty, an ear that longs for music, a mouth that longs for sweet flavours, ambitions and energies that crave fulfilment. Some few may live to eighty years, some fewer to a hundred; but one who lives till sixty has still not died young. And during these sixty years, if we take away the time that is spent in sickness, mourning and trouble, in all this time there will not be more than four or five days in each month when his lips are opened and laughter comes.

'Heaven and earth are illimitable; to man a term is set. Furnished only with the scrap of time that is his span, he is committed to a place amid the illimitables. A flash, and all is over, like a racehorse seen through a crack. He who by the enjoyment of his senses can use this brief moment to the full alone can claim to have found the Way. All that you acclaim, I utterly discard. Be off with you as fast as you can, and never dare prate to me again! This Way of yours is nothing but noise and babble, humbug and empty fraud, such as could never help any man to perfect the unalloyed that is within him; is in fact not worth a moment's discussion.' Confucius prostrated himself twice, and retired at full speed. When he had reached the gate of the camp and regained his carriage, his hands were trembling to such an extent that three times the reins fell out of them, there was a cloud before his eyes and his face was ashen grey. He leant over the fore-rail with sunken head, gasping for breath. At last he reached Lu, and outside the eastern gate happened to meet Liu-hsia Hui. 'What has become of you lately?' asked Liu-hsia Hui. 'I have not seen you for several days. Judging by the appearance of your horses and carriage, I should think you have been on a journey. Is it possible that, despite my warning, you have been to see my brother Chih?' Confucius gazed upwards at the sky and sighed. 'I have indeed,' he said. 'And Chih,' said Liu-hsia Hui, 'did not take to your ideas any more kindly than I predicted?' 'That is true,' said Confucius. 'I must confess that, as the saying goes, I poulticed myself with moxa when there was nothing wrong with me. I rushed off to dress a tiger's head and plait its beard. Small wonder if I nearly landed in the tiger's maw!'

There is a somewhat similar story in another collection of Taoist writings, *Lieh Tzu*. This time a sage is grieved by the conduct not of one but of two brothers whose philosophy, though they are plain voluptuaries, not brigands, is identical with that of the robber Chih:

When Tzu-ch'an was Prime Minister of Chêng and the government of the country had been entirely in his control for three years, the good citizens gladly accepted all his reforms and the bad citizens dared not transgress his prohibitions. Order prevailed everywhere in the State, and the neighbouring princes treated Chêng with proper respect.

But Tzu-ch'an had an elder brother named Kung-sun Chao and a younger brother named Kung-sun Mu. Chao loved wine and Mu loved beauty. In Chao's house were stored countless gallons of wine, and hillocks of yeast[1] lay heaped there, so that the nose of anyone coming to see him was assailed by a smell of lees and liquor at a hundred paces from his door. So reckless did he become under the influence of wine that he no longer knew whether the world was at peace or at war, whether the principles of humanity were safe or at stake, whether his household was intact or lost, which of his kin were near and which distant; nor, as between preservation and extinction, which was a matter for grief and which for rejoicing. Though flood, fire, or sword-blade threatened him with instant destruction, he paid no heed.

Meanwhile in the back courtyards of his brother Mu were lined up apartments by the score, all filled with young girls of exquisite beauty, chosen with the utmost care. And so utterly did he immerse himself in the pleasure of love that he had no time to receive even his nearest relations, gave up all friendly meetings and excursions, and would remain ensconced in his back premises continuing the business of night far into the day, sometimes for three months on end without ever once coming out. But even so, he remained unsatisfied, and if it was reported that in any district there was an unmarried girl of particular beauty, he sent gifts and summoned her, or used a go-between to procure her; nor did success in one such enterprise prevent him from immediately embarking upon another.

The conduct of his brothers was a matter of constant concern to Tzu-ch'an. At last he went privately to the philosopher Têng Hsi and asked for his advice. 'I have heard,' he said, 'that he who would govern a family must first learn governance of self, and that he who would govern a land must learn to govern a family. By this it is evidently meant that the process should proceed

[1] For making more wine, i.e. rice-beer.

from near to far. Now although I have established good government in this land, my family is in disorder. It would seem, therefore, that I have begun at the wrong end. Can you suggest any means of saving my two relatives from their evil ways? I wish you would tell me.' 'This situation,' replied Têng Hsi, 'has long astonished me; but I did not like to broach the matter. You should certainly put things straight while there is still time. Surely you can point out to them the supreme value of a constitution unimpaired, the deep importance of manners and morals?' Acting on Têng Hsi's advice, Tzu-ch'an found a suitable opportunity to visit his brothers, and said to them: 'What makes man superior to birds and beasts is possession of reason and foresight. Reason and foresight lead to manners and morals. When manners and morals are cultivated, reputation and rank are sure to follow. Whereas if a man allows himself to act merely according to the feelings of moment, abandoning himself to every lust and desire, his constitution, moral and physical, is bound to suffer. I can promise you that if you take my advice, the effect will be immediate. You have but to repent at dawn and by nightfall you will be enjoying opulent salaries.' 'You tell us nothing,' replied Chao and Mu, 'of which we have not long been aware. But our choice in the matter was also made long ago. It is strange to suppose that we were waiting for you to enlighten us. Life is of all things the hardest to meet with, and death the easiest to encounter. To degrade life, so hard to come by, to a level below death, so easy to encounter, is a course that, to say the least of it, could not be embarked upon without reflection. You recommend that by deference to morals and manners we should pander to the world, by doing violence to our natural desires should court reputation. But in our view death itself would be far preferable to such a life as you propose.

'All we desire is to get as much happiness as a single existence can give, to extract from each year as it passes the utmost pleasure that it can afford. Our only trouble is that the belly can hold no more while the mouth is still greedy, that the powers of the body give out while lust is still strong. We have no time to worry about such questions as whether our conduct is injurious to our worldly reputations or dangerous to our constitutions. Thinking that the ability to govern a country implies the power to bend all creatures to your will, you come to us convinced that your fine speeches will upset all our ideas, your promises of rank and salary will fill us with delight. Are not such tricks mean and truly pitiable? We for our part should like once more to define our position to you. He who is bent upon putting the world around him in order cannot be certain that the world will accept his rule, but may be sure that his own life will be disagreeable. He who is bent only upon enjoying life cannot be certain that the world will therefore be disordered, but he may be sure that he himself will be a great deal more comfortable. Your method, with its insistence on what lies without, may be made to work for a short time and in a single State. But it is at variance with the inclinations of mankind. Whereas our principle, that of attending to what is within, if it could be extended to every land under Heaven, would do away in the end with any need for government. We have always thought that you needed instruction in this doctrine, and it is strange that you should now come and force upon us that contrary doctrine of yours!'

Tzu-ch'an felt completely at a loss, and could make no reply. Next day he told Têng Hsi what had happened. 'You have had True Sages in your family,' said Têng Hsi, 'without ever being aware of it. How, I wonder, did you come by your reputation as a wise man? The fact that there is good order in Chêng must be a mere accident; it certainly can be no doing of yours.'

Death

I have already translated a passage concerning the death of Chuang Tzu's wife. His attitude towards death, exemplified again and again in the book, 'is but part of a general attitude towards the universal laws of nature, which is one not merely of resignation nor even of acquiescence, but a lyrical, almost ecstatic acceptance, which has inspired some of the most moving passages in Taoist literature.'[1] I have here collected one or two further passages about death.

When Chuang Tzu was going to Ch'u he saw by the roadside a skull, clean and bare, but with every bone in its place. Touching it gently with his chariot-whip he bent over it and asked it saying, 'Sir, was it some insatiable ambition that drove you to transgress the law and brought you to this? Was it the fall of a kingdom, the blow of an executioner's axe that brought you to this? Or had you done some shameful deed and could not face the reproaches of father and mother, of wife and child, and so were brought to this? Was it hunger and cold that brought you to this, or was it that the springs and autumns of your span had in their due course carried you to this?'

Having thus addressed the skull, he put it under his head as a pillow and went to sleep. At midnight the skull appeared to him in a dream and said to him, 'All that you said to me—your glib, commonplace chatter—is just what I should expect from a live man, showing as it does in every phrase a mind hampered by tram-

[1] The Way and Its Power.

mels from which we dead are entirely free. Would you like to hear a word or two about the dead?'

'I certainly should,' said Chuang Tzu.

'Among the dead,' said the skull, 'none is king, none is subject, there is no division of the seasons; for us the whole world is spring, the whole world is autumn. No monarch on his throne has joy greater than ours.'

Chuang Tzu did not believe this. 'Suppose,' he said, 'I could get the Clerk of Destinies to make your frame anew, to clothe your bones once more with flesh and skin, send you back to father and mother, wife and child, friends and home, I do not think you would refuse.'

A deep frown furrowed the skeleton's brow. 'How can you imagine,' it asked, 'that I would cast away joy greater than that of a king upon his throne, only to go back again to the toils of the living world?'

Tzu-lai fell ill. He was already at the last gasp; his wife and children stood weeping and wailing round his bed. 'Pst,' said Tzu-li, who had come to call, 'stand back! A great Change is at work; let us not disturb it.' Then, leaning against the door, he said to Tzu-lai, 'Mighty are the works of the Changer! What is he about to make of you, to what use will he put you? Perhaps a rat's liver, perhaps a beetle's claw!' 'A child,' said Tzu-lai, 'at its parents' bidding must go north and south, east or west; how much the more when those parents of all Nature, the great powers Yin and Yang command him, must he needs go where they will. They have asked me to die, and if I do not obey them, shall I not rank as an unmanageable child? I can make no complaint against them. These great forces housed me in my bodily frame, spent me in youth's toil, gave me repose when I was old, will give me rest at my death. Why should the powers that have done so much for me in life, do less for me in death?

'If the bronze in the founder's crucible were suddenly

to jump up and say, "I don't want to be a tripod, a plough-share or a bell. I must be the sword *Without Flaw*," the caster would think it was indeed unmannerly metal that had got into his stock.

'In this life I have had the luck to be fashioned in human form. But were I now to say to the Great Transformer, "I refuse to let anything be made out of me but a man," he would think that it was indeed an unmannerly being who had come into his hands.'

How do I know that wanting to be alive is not a great mistake? How do I know that hating to die is not like thinking one has lost one's way, when all the time one is on the path that leads to home? Li Chi was the daughter of the frontier guardsman at Ai. When first she was captured and carried away to Chin, she wept till her dress was soaked with tears. But when she came to the king's palace, sat with him on his couch and shared with him the dainties of the royal board, she began to wonder why she had wept. How do I know that the dead do not wonder why they should ever have prayed for long life? It is said that those who dream of drinking wine will weep when day comes; and that those who dream of weeping will next day go hunting. But while a man is dreaming, he does not know that he is dreaming; nor can he interpret a dream till the dream is done. It is only when he wakes, that he knows it was a dream. Not till the Great Wakening can he know that all this was one Great Dream. . . .

Once Chuang Chou[1] dreamt that he was a butterfly. He did not know that he had ever been anything but a butterfly and was content to hover from flower to flower. Suddenly he woke and found to his astonishment that he was Chuang Chou. But it was hard to be sure whether he really was Chou and had only dreamt that he was a butterfly, or was really a butterfly, and was only dreaming that he was Chou.

[1] I.e. Chuang Tzu.

The Cicada and the Wren

There is a theme in Chuang Tzu which he himself
calls the Cicada and the Wren. You will understand
immediately the nature of this theme if I translate
for you the fable from which it takes its name. There
are birds that fly many hundred miles without a halt.
Someone mentioned this to the cicada and the wren,
who agreed that such a thing was impossible. 'You
and I know very well,' they said, 'that the furthest
one can ever get even by the most tremendous effort
is that elm-tree over there; and even this one cannot
be sure of reaching every time. Often one finds oneself dragged back to earth long before one gets there.
All these stories about flying hundreds of miles at a
stretch are sheer nonsense.'

The same theme recurs in the most famous of all
Chuang Tzu's allegories, the chapter called The
Autumn Flood.

It was the time when the autumn floods come down.
A hundred streams swelled the River, that spread and
spread till from shore to shore, nay from island to island
so great was the distance that one could not tell horse
from bull. The god of the River felt extremely pleased
with himself. It seemed to him that all lovely things
under heaven had submitted to his power. He wandered
down-stream, going further and further to the east, till
at last he came to the sea. He gazed eastwards, confidently expecting to see the further shore. He could dis-
cern no end to the waters. Then the god of the River
began to turn his head, peering this way and that; but

still he could see no shore. At last, addressing the ocean, he said with a deep sigh: 'There is a proverb which says,

> None like me
> Proves none so blind as he.

I fear it applies very well to myself . . . as I realize only too well when I gaze at your limitless immensity. Had I not this day enrolled myself as your disciple, I might well have made myself the laughing-stock of all who take the Wider View.'

Kung-sun Lung[1] said to the recluse, Prince Mou of Wei, 'When I was young I studied the Way of the Former Kings; when I grew up, I became versed in the dictates of goodness and duty. From the dialecticians I learnt how to blend identity and difference, the so and the not-so, the possible and the impossible. I exhausted the wisdom of the Hundred Schools, could confute the arguments of countless mouths, and believed that I had nothing left to learn. But recently I heard Chuang Tzu speaking, and was reduced to helpless amazement. I do not know why it was—perhaps the right arguments did not occur to me, perhaps he really knows more than I do. But in any case, "my beak was jammed"; I had not a word to say. Please tell me how one deals with him.' Prince Mou leant over his arm-rest and heaved a deep sigh, then looked up to Heaven and laughed aloud saying, 'Do you not know the story of the frog that lived in the abandoned[2] well? "How you must envy my delightful existence!" it said to the giant turtle of the Eastern Sea. "When I feel inclined I can come out and hop about on the railing; then I go back into the pit and rest where a tile has fallen out of the wall. When I go into the water I can make it hold me up under the arm-pits and support

---

[1] A famous pacifist and dialectician; lived c. 300 B.C.
[2] Abandoned because it had dried up.

my chin; when I jump into the mud, I can make it bury my feet and cover my ankles. As for the baby crabs and tadpoles, none of them can compete with me. To have the use of all the waters of an entire pool, to have at one's command all the delights of a disused well, that surely is the most that life can give. Why don't you, just as an experiment, come down here and see for yourself?"

'The giant turtle of the Eastern Sea attempted to get into the well; but before its left foot was well in, its right foot had got wedged fast. Whereupon it wriggled itself free and retreated, saying, "As you have been kind enough to tell me about your well, allow me to tell you about the sea. Imagine a distance of a thousand leagues, and you will still have no idea of its size; imagine a height of a thousand times man's stature, and you will still have no notion of its depth. In the time of the Great Yü, in ten years there were nine floods; but the sea became no deeper. In the time of T'ang the Victorious there were seven years of drought in eight years; yet the sea did not retreat from its shores. Not to be harried by the moments that flash by nor changed by the ages that pass; to receive much, yet not increase, to receive little, yet not diminish, this is the Great Joy of the Eastern Sea."

'Knowledge such as yours gives no standard by which to set the boundaries between false and true; yet you take it upon yourself to scrutinize Chuang Tzu's teaching. As well might a gnat try to carry the Great Mountain on its back or an ant try to change the course of the River. The task is utterly beyond your powers.

'Priding yourself upon a wisdom that is unable to confute the transcendant mysteries of Chuang Tzu's doctrine merely because your cleverness has brought you a few short-lived victories, are you not indeed a Frog in the Well?

'Thoughts such as his, that can cross the Dark Streams of death, mount to the Royal Empyrean, that know neither east nor west, south nor north, but plunge into the bottomless chasm; thoughts from which all boundaries have loosened and dropped away, that begin in the Secret Darkness, that go back to the time when all was one—how can you hope to reach them by the striving of a petty intelligence or ransack them by the light of your feeble sophistries? You might as well look at Heaven through a reed or measure earth with the point of a gimlet. Your instruments are too small.

'Be off with you! But before you go I should like to remind you of what happened to the child from Shou-ling that was sent to Han-tan to learn the "Han-tan Walk." He failed to master the steps, but spent so much time in trying to acquire them that in the end he forgot how one usually walks, and came home to Shou-ling crawling on all fours.

'I advise you to keep away; or you will forget what you know already and find yourself without a trade.'

Kung-sun Lung's mouth gaped and would not close; his tongue stuck to the roof of his mouth and would not go down. He made off as fast as his legs would carry him.

Yoga

We have seen Lao Tzu sitting 'so utterly motionless that one could not believe a human being was there at all,' 'stark and lifeless as a withered tree.' Another Taoist adept, Nan-kuo Tzu Ch'i, was observed by his pupil Yen-ch'êng Tzu Yu to be sitting with his face turned upwards to Heaven, breathing gently through parted lips,[1] motionless as a ploughman whose mate has left him. 'What is this?' said Yen-ch'êng Tzu Yu.

[1] The word here used became in later Taoism the technical name of one of the six forms of expiration; see H. Maspero, *Journal Asiatique*, July–September 1937, p. 248 seq.

'Can limbs indeed be made to become as a withered tree, can the heart indeed be made to become as dead ashes? What is now propped upon that stool is not he that a little while ago propped himself upon that stool.'[1] It is evident that in these two passages some kind of trance-state is being described. But the language is conventional and imprecise. Much the same description is given of a man concentrated upon a practical task,[2] and again of a man asleep.[3] It is possible that many commonplace words had, in connection with mystic practices, a technical sense which now escapes us. One common and ordinary word, yu, 'to wander, to travel,' which in Confucian circles had the technical meaning 'to go from Court to Court as a peripatetic counsellor,'[4] had for the Taoists a very different meaning.

In the beginning[5] Lieh Tzu was fond of travelling. The adept Hu-ch'iu Tzu said to him, 'I hear that you are fond of travelling. What is it in travelling that pleases you?' 'For me,' said Lieh Tzu, 'the pleasure of travelling consists in the appreciation of variety. When some people travel they merely contemplate what is before their eyes; when I travel, I contemplate the processes of mutability.' 'I wonder,' said Hu-ch'iu Tzu, 'whether your travels are not very much the same as other people's, despite the fact that you think them so different. Whenever people look at anything, they are necessarily looking at processes of change, and one may well appreciate the mutability of outside things, while wholly unaware of one's own muta-

[1] II. a.
[2] XIX. c.
[3] XXII. c.
[4] Cf. Mencius VII. 1, IX. 1.
[5] I.e. before his conversion. See Lieh Tzu, IV. g.

bility. Those who take infinite trouble about external travels, have no idea how to set about the sight-seeing[1] that can be done within. The traveller abroad is dependent upon outside things; he whose sightseeing is inward, can in himself find all he needs. Such is the highest form of travelling; while it is a poor sort of journey that is dependent upon outside things.'

After this Lieh Tzu never went anywhere at all, aware that till now he had not known what travelling means. 'Now,' said Hu-chi'iu Tzu, 'you may well become a traveller indeed! The greatest traveller does not know where he is going; the greatest sight-seer does not know what he is looking at. His travels do not take him to one part of creation more than another; his sight-seeing is not directed to one sight rather than another. That is what I mean by true sight-seeing. And that is why I said, "Now you may well become a traveller indeed!" '

Yu, then, in its Taoist acceptation, is a spiritual not a bodily journey. There is naturally a constant play between these two senses of the word.

Shih-nan I-liao visited the lord of Lu, and found him looking sad. 'Why do you look so sad?' he asked. 'I study the Way of former kings,' said the lord of Lu, 'carry on the work of my ancestors, humble myself before the spirits of the dead, give honour to the wise. All this I do in my own person, never for a moment abating in my zeal. Yet troubles beset my reign. That is why I am sad.' 'My lord,' said Shih-nan I-liao, 'your method of avoiding troubles is a superficial one. The bushy-coated fox and the striped panther, though they lodge deep in the mountain woods, hide in caverns on the cliff-side, go out at night but stay at home all day, and even when driven desperate by thirst and hunger

---

[1] The word is applied to looking at waterfalls, views, etc.; but also to mystic contemplation.

keep always far from the rivers and lakes where food might easily be had—despite their quietness, caution, and the mastery of their desires, do not escape misfortune, but fall an easy prey to the trapper's net and snare. And this, not through any fault of theirs; it is the value of their fur that brings them to disaster. And in your case, my lord, is it not the land of Lu itself that is your lordship's fur, and the cause of your undoing?

'I would have you strip away not your fine fur only, but every impediment of the body, scour your heart till it is free from all desire, and travel through the desolate wilds. For to the south there is a place called the Land where Tê Rules. Its people are ignorant and unspoiled, negligent of their own interests, and of few desires. They know how to make, but do not know how to hoard. They give, but seek no return. The suitabilities of decorum, the solemnities of ritual are alike unknown to them. They live and move thoughtlessly and at random, yet every step they take tallies with the Great Plan. They know how to enjoy life while it lasts, are ready to be put away when death comes.

'I would have you leave your kingdom and its ways, take Tao as your guide and travel to this land.'

'It is a long way to go,' said the prince of Lu, 'and dangerous. There are rivers too swift for any boat, mountains that no chariot can cross. What am I to do?' 'Humility,' said Shih-nan I-liao, 'shall be your boat. Pliancy shall be your chariot.' 'It is a long way to go,' said the prince, 'and the lands through which it passes are not inhabited. There would be no villages where I could buy provisions or take a meal. I should die long before I reached my journey's end.' 'Lessen your wants, husband your powers,' said Shih-nan I-liao, 'and you will have no need to buy provisions on your way. You will cross many rivers and come at last to a lake so wide that, gaze as you will, you cannot see the further shore. Yet you will go on, without knowing whether it will ever end. At the shores of this lake all that came

with you will turn back. But you will still have far to go.
What matter? "He who needs others is for ever shackled;
he who is needed by others is for ever sad." . . . I would
have you drop these shackles, put away your sadness,
and wander alone with Tao in the kingdom of the Great
Void.'

King Mu and the Wizard

In the time of king Mu of Chou there came from a
land in the far west a wizard who could go into water
and fire, pierce metals and stone, turn mountains upside
down, make rivers flow backwards, move fortifications
and towns, ride on the air without falling, collide with
solids without injury. There was indeed no limit to the
miracles that he could perform. And not only could he
change the outward shape of material things; he could
also transform the thoughts of men. King Mu reverenced
him like a god, served him like a master, put his own
State chambers at the wizard's disposal, gave him for
sustenance the animals reared for Imperial sacrifice, and
for his entertainment chose girls skilled in music and
dancing.

But the wizard found the king's palace too cramped
and sordid to live in; the choicest delicacies from the
king's kitchen he pronounced to be coarse and rancid,
and he would not eat them. The ladies from the king's
harem he would not look at, so foul and hideous did he
find them.

The king accordingly set about building a completely
new palace, employing all the most skilful workers in
clay and wood, the most accomplished decorators in
whitewash and ochre; expending indeed so much upon
the work that by the time it was complete all his Treas-

uries were empty. The towers were six thousand feet
high, and from them one looked down upon the top
of the Chung-nan hills. It was named The Tower
that hits Heaven. The king chose, from among the vir-
gins of Chêng and Wei, girls of the most transcendant
beauty and charm, anointed them with fragrant oils,
straightened the curve of their eyebrows, decked them
with combs and ear-rings, clothed them in jackets of the
softest gauze, skirts of the thinnest floss, beautified them
with white powder and with black, set jade rings at their
girdles, strewed the floors with scented herbs, and
brought these ladies to the palace till it was full. For
the wizard's pleasure continual music was played, Receiv-
ing the Clouds, The Six Gems, The Nine Songs of
Succession, The Morning Dew; every month he received
a supply of costly garments, and every morning he was
provided with costly food. But he was still far from
content and could only with the greatest difficulty be
persuaded to approach this new abode. After some time
had passed, during which the magician frequently absented himself, he one day invited the king to accom-
pany him upon a journey. Whereupon the magician
began to rise from the ground and the king, clutching
at his sleeve, was carried up and up, till they reached the
sky. Here they halted, just in front of the magician's
house, which was moated with dust of silver and gold
and looped with festoons of jade and pearl. It stood out
far above the rain and clouds. What it rested upon was
hard to say, but it seemed to be supported by a coil of
cloud. In this house nothing that his ears and eyes heard
or saw, nothing that his nose and mouth smelt or tasted
was in the least like what the king was accustomed to in
the world of men. This, he thought, must surely be
Stainless City, Purple Mystery, Level Sky, Wide Joy—
one of the palaces of God. Looking down at the world
below he saw what seemed like a hummock in the
ground, with some piles of brushwood lying around it,
and suddenly realized that this was his own palace with

its arbours. Here as it seemed to him he lived for twenty
or thirty years without a thought for his kingdom. At
last the wizard again invited him to make a journey,
and once more they travelled, till they had reached a
place where looking up one could not see the sun or
moon, looking down one saw neither river nor lake. So
fierce a light blazed and flashed that the king's eyes
were dazzled and he could not look; so loud a noise
jangled and echoed that his ears were deafened and he
could not listen. His limbs loosened, his entrails were as
though dissolved within him, his thoughts were confused, his energy extinct. 'Let us go back,' he cried to
the wizard, who gave him a push and soon they were
falling through space.

The next thing that he knew was that he was sitting
just where he had sat when the magician summoned
him; the same attendants were still at his side, the wine
that they had just served to him was still warm, the food
still moist. 'Where have I been?' he asked. 'Your
Majesty,' one of his servants answered, 'has been sitting
there in silence.'

It was three days before the king was completely
himself again. On his recovery he sent for the wizard
and asked him to explain what had happened. 'I took
you,' the wizard replied, 'upon a journey of the soul.
Your body never moved. The place where you have
been living was none other than your own palace; the
grounds in which you strolled were in fact your own
park.

'Your Majesty, between himself and the understanding of such things, interposes habitual doubts. Could
you for a moment divest yourself of them, there is no
miracle of mine, no trick with time, that you could not
imitate.'

The king was very pleased, paid no further heed to
affairs of State, amused himself no more with ministers
or concubines, but devoted himself henceforth to distant
journeys of the soul.

Yang-shêng

Yang-shêng, 'nurturing life,' that is to say conserving one's vital powers, is often divided by the later Taoists into four branches, (1) The Secrets of the Chamber, which enabled the Yellow Ancestor to enjoy twelve hundred concubines without injury to his health; (2) Breath Control; (3) the physical exercises[1] which, as in Indian *hatha* yoga, were associated with breath control; (4) Diet.

By some early Taoists, as we shall see, such practices were regarded as yang-hsing, 'nurturing the bodily frame,' not as yang-shêng, which to them implied an attitude towards life rather than a system of hygiene.

To have strained notions and stilted ways of behaviour, to live apart from the world and at variance with the common ways of men, to hold lofty discourse, full of resentment and scorn, to have no aim but superiority—such is the wont of the hermit in his mountain recess, of the man in whose eyes the world is always wrong, of those that shrivel in the summer heat or cast themselves into the seething pool.

To talk of goodness and duty, loyalty and faithfulness, respect, frugality, promoting the advancement of others to the detriment of one's own, to seek no end but moral perfection—such is the wont of those who would set the world in order, men of admonition and instruction, educators itinerant or at home.

[1] To the bird-stretchings and bear-hangings mentioned below a compilation of the 2nd century B.C. (*Huai-nan Tzu*, chap. 7) adds the Pigeon's Bath, the Monkey Dance, the Owl Gaze, the Tiger Regard.

To talk of mighty deeds, to achieve high fame, to assign to the ruler and his ministers the rites that each is to perform, to graduate the functions of the high and low, to care for public matters and these alone—such is the wont of those that frequent tribunal and court, of those whose only end is the aggrandizement of their master, the strengthening of his domain, who think only of victories and annexations.

To seek out some thicket or swamp, remain in the wilderness, hook fish in a quiet place, to seek no end but inactivity—such is the wont of wanderers by river and lake, of those that shun the world, of those whose quest is idleness alone. To pant, to puff, to hail, to sip,[1] to cast out the old breath and induct the new, bear-hangings and bird-stretchings, with no aim but long life—such is the wont of the Inducer, nurturer of the bodily frame, aspirant to P'êng Tsu's high longevity.

But there are those whose thoughts are sublime without being strained; who have never striven after goodness, yet are perfect. There are those who win no victories for their State, achieve no fame, and yet perfect its policies; who find quietness, though far from streams and lakes; who live to great old age, though they have never practised Induction (tao-yin). They have divested themselves of everything, yet lack nothing. They are passive, seek no goal; but all lovely things attend them. Such is the way of Heaven and Earth, the secret power of the Wise. Truly is it said, 'Quietness, stillness, emptiness, not-having, inactivity—these are the balancers of Heaven and Earth, the very substance of the Way and its Power.' Truly is it said, 'The Wise Man rests therein, and because he rests, he is at peace. Because he is at peace, he is quiet.' One who is at peace and is quiet no sorrow or harm can enter, no evil breath can invade. Therefore his inner power remains whole and his spirit intact.

Truly is it said, 'For the Wise Man life is conformity

[1] Technical names of breathing exercises.

to the motions of Heaven, death is but part of the common law of Change. At rest, he shares the secret powers of Yin; at work, he shares the rocking of the waves of Yang. He neither invites prosperity nor courts disaster. Only when incited does he respond, only when pushed does he move, only as a last resort will he rise. He casts away all knowledge and artifice, follows the pattern of Heaven. Therefore Heaven visits him with no calamity, the things of the world do not lay their trammels upon him, no living man blames him, no ghost attacks him. His life is like the drifting of a boat, his death is like a lying down to rest. He has no anxieties, lays no plans.

'He is full of light, yet none is dazzled; he is faithful, yet bound by no promise. His sleep is without dreams, his waking without grief. His spirit has remained stainless and unspoiled; his soul (*hun*) has not grown weary. Emptiness, nothingness, quiet—these have made him partner in the powers of Heaven.'

Truly it is said, 'Sadness and joy are the perverters of the Inner Power; delight and anger are offences against the Way; love and hate are sins against the Power. Therefore when the heart neither grieves nor rejoices, the Power is at its height. To be one thing and not to change, is the climax of stillness. To have nothing in one that resists, is the climax of emptiness. To remain detached from all outside things, is the climax of fineness.[1] To have in oneself no contraries, is the climax of purity.'[2]

Truly is it said, 'If the bodily frame of a man labours and has no rest, it wears itself out; if his spiritual essence is used without cessation, then it flags, and having flagged, runs dry.

'The nature of water is that if nothing is mixed with it, it remains clear; if nothing ruffles it, it remains

[1] *T'an*, the opposite of 'grossness.'
[2] In the sense of 'unmixedness.'

smooth. But if it is obstructed so that it does not flow, then too it loses its clearness. In these ways it is a symbol of the heavenly powers that are in man.'

Truly is it said, 'A purity unspoiled by any contamination, a peace and unity not disturbed by any variation, detachment and inactivity broken only by such movement as is in accord with the motions of Heaven—such are the secrets that conserve the soul. Does not he who possesses a sword of Kan or Yüeh put it in a case and hide it away, not daring to make use of it? A greater treasure still is the soul. It can glide hither and thither where it will. There is no point in Heaven above to which it cannot climb, no hollow in the earth into which it cannot crawl. It infuses and transforms the ten thousand creatures. For it there is no symbol; its name is "One with God" (*Ti*).

> 'Only the way of wholeness and integrity
> Can guard the soul.
> Guard it so that nothing is lost,
> And you will become one with the soul.
> The essence of this "one," blending,
> Will mingle with Heaven's law.'

It is of this that a rustic saying speaks, which says:

> The crowd cares for gain,
> The honest man for fame,
> The good man values success,
> But the Wise Man, his soul.

Therefore we talk of his simplicity, meaning that he keeps his soul free from all admixture; and of his wholeness, meaning that he keeps it intact and entire. He that can achieve such wholeness, such integrity we call a True Man.

The third chapter of *Chuang Tzu* is called 'Principles of Life Nurture.' It is extremely short and scrappy, and would appear to have been mutilated. Of its three anecdotes only the first seems to be directly concerned with yang-shêng:

King Hui of Wei had a carver named Ting. When this carver Ting was carving a bull for the king, every touch of the hand, every inclination of the shoulder, every step he trod, every pressure of the knee, while swiftly and lightly he wielded his carving-knife, was as carefully timed as the movements of a dancer in the *Mulberry Wood*. . . . 'Wonderful,' said the king. 'I could never have believed that the art of carving could reach such a point as this.' 'I am a lover of Tao,' replied Ting, putting away his knife, 'and have succeeded in applying it to the art of carving. When I first began to carve I fixed my gaze on the animal in front of me. After three years I no longer saw it as a whole bull, but as a thing already divided into parts. Nowadays I no longer see it with the eye; I merely apprehend it with the soul. My sense-organs are in abeyance, but my soul still works. Unerringly my knife follows the natural markings, slips into the natural cleavages, finds its way into the natural cavities. And so by conforming my work to the structure with which I am dealing, I have arrived at a point at which my knife never touches even the smallest ligament or tendon, let alone the main gristle.

'A good carver changes his knife once a year; by which time the blade is dented. An ordinary carver changes it once a month; by which time it is broken. I have used my present knife for nineteen years, and during that time have carved several thousand bulls. But the blade still looks as though it had just come out of the mould. Where part meets part there is always space, and a knife-blade has no thickness. Insert an instrument that has no thickness into a structure that is amply spaced, and surely it cannot fail to have plenty of room. That is why I can use a blade for nineteen years, and yet it still looks as though it were fresh from the forger's mould.

'However, one has only to look at an ordinary carver to see what a difficult business he finds it. One sees how nervous he is while making his preparations, how long he looks, how slowly he moves. Then after some small, niggling strokes of the knife, when he has done no more than detach a few stray fragments from the whole, and even that by dint of continually twisting and turning like a worm burrowing through the earth, he stands back, with his knife in his hand, helplessly gazing this way and that, and after hovering for a long time finally curses a perfectly good knife and puts it back in its case.'

'Excellent,' said the king of Wei. 'This interview with the carver Ting has taught me how man's vital forces can be conserved.'[1]

The Taoist, then, does not wear himself out by useless conflict with the unchangeable laws of existence; nor does he struggle to amend the unalterable tendencies of his own nature:

When Prince Mou of Wei was living as a hermit in Chung-shan,[2] he said to the Taoist Chan Tzu, 'My body is here amid lakes and streams; but my heart is in the palace of Wei. What am I to do?' 'Care more for what you have in yourself,' said Chan Tzu, 'and less for what you can get from others.' 'I know I ought to,' said the prince, 'but I cannot get the better of my feelings.' 'If you cannot get the better of your feelings,' replied Chan Tzu, 'then give play to them. Nothing is worse for the soul than struggling not to give play to feelings that it cannot control. This is called the Double Injury, and of those that sustain it none live out their natural span.'

[1] The text of this story is very corrupt; but the general sense is clear. I have followed the renderings of Chu Kuei-yao and Kao Hêng.

[2] In southern Hopei. Cf. two other versions of this story, in *Huai-nan Tzu*, XII, and *Lü Shih Ch'un Ch'iu*.

The Taoist and Tao

Chuang Tzu in various places gives descriptions, generally in verse, of the Master Taoist, 'the supreme man,' 'the true[1] man,' 'the man of supreme inward power.'

'The great bushlands are ablaze, but he feels no heat; the River and the Han stream are frozen over, but he feels no cold. Fierce thunders break the hills, winds rock the ocean, but he is not startled.'

'He can climb high and not stagger; go through water and not be wet, go through fire and not be scorched.'

'The great floods mount up to Heaven, but he is not drowned; the great drought melts metal and stone, burns fields and hills, but he is not singed.'

Lieh Tzu asked Kuan Yin, saying, ' "The Man of Extreme Power . . . can tread on fire without being burnt. Walk on the top of the whole world and not stagger." May I ask how he attains to this?' 'He is protected,' said Kuan Yin, 'by the purity of his breath. Knowledge and skill, determination and courage could never lead to this. . . . When a drunk man falls from his carriage, however fast it may be going, he is never killed. His bones and joints are not different from those of other men; but his susceptibility to injury is different from theirs. This is because his soul is intact.[2] He did

---

[1] Or 'pure man,' using pure not in the moral sense but as it is used in the expression 'pure gold.' Cf. the Hindu term Satpurusha.

[2] Is impervious to disturbances from outside.

not know that he was riding; he does not know that he
has fallen out. Neither death nor life, astonishment nor
fear can enter into his breast; therefore when he bumps
into things, he does not stiffen with fright. If such
integrity of the spirit can be got from wine, how much
greater must be the integrity that is got from Heaven?'

The above is a true Taoist passage. Whereas the
explanation of the Taoist's invulnerability put for-
ward in the famous *Autumn Flood* chapter (a strange
blend of sublimity and fatuity) is a feeble rationali-
zation: ' "Fire cannot burn him, water cannot drown
him, cold and heat cannot hurt him, wild animals
cannot harm him." This does not mean that he
exposes himself recklessly; it means that he is so
well versed in what is safe and what is dangerous,
. . . so cautious in shunning and approaching, that
nothing can do him injury.'

The idea that mystic practices can bring invulnerability, is also found in Hindu treatises on yoga:
'The *āmbhasī* is a great *mudrā*; the yogi who knows
it never meets death even in the deepest water.
Even if the practitioner is thrown into burning
fire, by virtue of this *mudrā* (the Āgneyī) he remains
alive.'[1] It is ideas of this kind that link the early
philosophic Taoism with the magical Taoism which
grew up in the second century A.D. and which even
at the end of the nineteenth inspired the leaders
of the Boxer Revolution with the belief that no
weapon could harm them.

The same kind of immunity is attributed to the
balian (wizards) of Indonesia and to medicine-men
in many parts of Africa, and we might be tempted
to suppose that Taoism was a sublimation of doc-

[1] Gheranda Samhitā, 73.

trines particularly connected with magicians analogous to the medicine-man or *balian*. The person, however, who played the role of wizard in ancient China was the *wu*, a dancing shaman, often but not always a woman. There is never any suggestion that the legendary Taoist saints were regarded as *wu*, and only one *wu* is mentioned in *Chuang Tzu*, a 'holy *wu*,' called Chi-hsien,[1] whose specialty was fortune-telling.[2]

Of course, if we regard Chuang Tzu as a philosopher and conceive of a philosopher as someone who presents the world with a rational alternative to 'superstition,' we shall be much upset by the passages which describe the Taoist's supernatural immunity. It has indeed often been suggested that the similar passage in the *Tao Tê Ching* (ch. 50) is a later interpolation.

If, on the other hand, we look upon magic, religion, and philosophy as ways of dealing with the same anxieties, we shall not be surprised to find these three sometimes overlapping, and shall not necessarily put the consolations of magic on a lower footing than those of philosophy or religion. Viewed from this standpoint the Taoist who believes that tigers cannot harm him is just as respectable a figure as the Idealist philosopher who fortifies himself by the belief that the universe consists solely of his own thoughts.

It may seem strange that, often though the term Tao appears in the foregoing pages, I have made no

[1] VII. e.

[2] In XIV. a, a person is mentioned whose name contains the element *wu*; but he does not figure as a shaman and the word may here be used only as a sort of surname, denoting that he was descended from a shaman.

attempt to explain what the Taoists meant by Tao.
I have purposely avoided doing so because I think
that a better idea of this can be got from the anecdotes that I have translated than from any attempt
at a definition. In *Chuang Tzu* there is, of course,
no systematic exposition of what Tao is; there are
only dithyrambic descriptions (chiefly in verse),
similar to those in the better known Taoist book
Tao Tê Ching, which I have translated in *The Way
and Its Power*. Here are one or two such passages:
'Tao is real, is faithful, yet does nothing and has
no form. Can be handed down, yet cannot be passed
from hand to hand, can be got but cannot be seen.
Is its own trunk, its own root.

'Before Heaven and Earth existed, from the beginning Tao was there. It is Tao that gave ghosts their
holy power (*shên*), that gave holy power to Dead
Kings. It gave life to Heaven, gave life to Earth. It
can mount above the Pole-star without becoming
high; it can sink below (the Springs of Death)
without becoming deep. It existed before Heaven
and Earth, yet has no duration; its age is greater
than that of the Longest Ago, yet it does not grow
old.

'Without it Heaven could not be high, Earth
could not be wide, the sun and moon could not
stay their course, the ten thousand things could
not flourish.'

In another passage (which unfortunately, owing
to corruption of the text, becomes unintelligible at
the end) we learn Tao is 'in the ant, in the broken
tile, in dung, in mire.' 'Do not seek precision,' says
Chuang Tzu, speaking of the realm of Tao. . . .
'I myself have traversed it this way and that; yet
still know only where it begins. I have roamed at

will through its stupendous spaces. I know how to get to them, but I do not know where they end.'

Dim Your Light

When Kêng-sang Ch'u, a pupil of Lao Tzu, went north and settled in Wei-lei, 'he would take no serving-man who betrayed any sign of intelligence nor engage any handmaiden who was in the least personable. The botchy and bloated shared his house, the dithering and fumbling waited upon him. After he had lived there for three years the crops in Wei-lei began to flourish marvellously. The people said to one another, "When he first came here, we thought him stupidly eccentric; but now the day is not long enough to count our blessings,[1] nay, the year is too short to hold them all. Certainly there must be a Sage among us, and perhaps it is he. Would it not be well if we planned together to set up a shrine where we could say our prayers to him and worship him as a god?" '

Kêng-sang, hearing of their intention to treat him as deity and ruler, was far from pleased. His disciples did not at all understand this. 'There is nothing in my attitude,' he said to them, 'which need surprise you. When the breath of spring is upon them, the hundred plants begin to grow; at the first coming of autumn, untold treasures mature. So long as the Great Way works unimpeded, spring and autumn cannot fail at their task. I have heard it said that where there is a Highest Man living among them the people herd blindly to their goal, ignorant of where they are going. But now it seems that the humble folk of Wei-lei have conceived the bright

[1] Cf. Book of Songs, p. 175 ('blessings so many that the day is not long enough for them all').

notion of setting me up on an altar, of ranging me among the Sages. Am I to consent to be a human sign-post? Were I to do so, I should indeed be unmindful of my master Lao Tzu's teaching.'

The story of Lao Tzu and Yang Tzu-chü, told above,[1] further illustrates the importance of seeming unimportant.

To be known is to be lost. The wise man 'hates that the crowd should come.' But to be known (like Colonel Lawrence) for your love of being unknown is to court a double notoriety:

Lieh Tzu set out for Ch'i, but turned back when he had only got half-way. 'Why did you start and then turn back again?' asked Po Hun Wu Jên, whom he chanced to meet on his return. 'I was upset by something that happened on the journey,' said Lieh Tzu. 'And what happened that upset you?' asked Po Hun Wu Jên. 'At five out of ten eating-houses where I went for food,' said Lieh Tzu, 'I was served before the other guests.' 'I do not see why that should have upset you,' said Po Hun Wu Jên. 'Because,' said Lieh Tzu, 'it meant that my inward perfection is not properly secured; its fiery light is leaking out through my bodily frame and turning men's thoughts astray, so that they defer to me in a way that gives offence to the honourable and aged and at the same time puts me in an unpleasant situation. True, an eating-housekeeper, trafficking in rice and soup, must lay in a stock greater than he can be sure of selling; his profits are necessarily small and his influence slight. But if even he can embarrass me in this way, how much the more am I in danger from such a one as the ruler of Ch'i, with his ten thousand war-chariots! He, no doubt, is worn out with the cares of national govern-ment, at his wits' end how to cope with all the business

[1] Page 17.

that confronts him. If I were to arrive in Ch'i he would at once load me with business, entrust me with all the most difficult tasks. That is why I was upset.' 'An admirable point of view,' said Po Hun Wu Jên. 'Persist in it and you will soon have disciples!'

Not long afterwards he called upon Lieh Tzu, and sure enough, there was a long row of shoes outside the door. Po Hun Wu Jên halted facing the door, planted his staff in the ground and rested his chin upon it, and after a while, without saying anything, he went away. The door-keeper told Lieh Tzu, who snatching up his slippers and carrying them in his hand ran barefoot to the door, and called out after Po Hun Wu Jên, 'As you are here, I hope, Sir, you will not go away without administering your dose.' 'It is all over,' said Po Hun Wu Jên. 'I told you before that you would soon have disciples, and now you have got them! It is not that you have been successful in attracting the attention of the world, but that you have been unsuccessful in distracting it. What good can they possibly do you? No man can be both admired and at peace. It is evident that you have aroused admiration, and this admiration (it goes without saying) has worked havoc upon your true nature. Remember the saying:

> 'Those who seek your society
> Tell you nothing;
> Such small talk as they bring
> Is but poison.
> Where none enlightens, none illumines,
> How can wisdom ripen?'

Buried among the People

There are those who 'betake themselves to thickets and swamps, seek their dwelling in desert spaces,

fish with a hook or sit all day doing nothing at all';
but the Taoist knows how to live in the world without being of the world, how to be at leisure without
the solitude of 'hills and seas.' If he 'buries himself
away' it is as a commoner among the common
people.

When Confucius was going to Ch'u, he lodged at an
eating-house in I-ch'iu. In the house next door there was
a man and his wife with menservants and maidservants.
. . . 'Who are all these people?' Tzu-lu asked of Confucius. 'They are the servants of a Sage,' said Confucius.
'Their master is one who has buried himself away among
the common people, hidden himself among the rice-
fields. His fame is extinct, but the sublimity of his disposition is unabated. His mouth still speaks; but his heart
has long since ceased to speak. He found himself at
variance with the world, and his heart no longer deigns
to consort with it. He is one who walking on dry land
is as though he were at the bottom of a pool. I wonder
if it is Shih-nan I-liao?' 'I will go and invite him to visit
us,' said Tzu-lu. 'Do nothing of the kind,' said Confucius. 'He knows that I have recognized him and will
be sure that when I get to Ch'u I shall persuade the king
of Ch'u to send for him. He looks upon me as a clever
intriguer; and such a man as that, so far from desiring
to meet such an intriguer, hates even to hear him speak.
How can you imagine that you will find him still there?'
Tzu-lu decided to go and look. It was as Confucius said;
the house next door had been suddenly evacuated.

The Shih-nan I-liao (I-liao South of the Market)
of the above story[1] had good reason to fear that his
peace might be disturbed. In 479 B.C. Po-kung Shêng

[1] We have already seen how he tried to convert the duke
of Lu to Taoism.

and Shih Ch'i were plotting to murder the two chief ministers of Ch'u. 'To deal with the king of Ch'u and the two ministers,' said Shêng, 'we need five hundred men.' 'I don't know where we can get them from,' said Shih Ch'i. 'We ought to get hold of Shih-nan I-liao,' said Shêng; 'that would be worth as much to us as five hundred men.' So he and Shih Ch'i went off to see I-liao, had some talk with him and were both very pleased. They told him of their plot, but he refused to take part in it. They then held a sword at his throat; but he remained entirely unmoved. Shih Ch'i wanted to kill him, fearing that he would reveal the plot. But Shêng said, 'Let him go. A man that cannot be cajoled by promises of gain nor scared by show of force will not let out our secret merely in order to win favour with the king.' According to one version of the story I-liao was playing ball when the conspirators threatened to kill him, and went on calmly doing so while the sword was at his throat.

A whole chapter of *Chuang Tzu*, the 28th, is devoted to stories of sages who refused the honours that monarchs importunately thrust upon them. These stories have no specifically Taoist character and almost all of them occur elsewhere in the literature of the period. The *Autumn Flood* chapter contains a story much more pointedly told, concerning Chuang Tzu himself.

When Chuang Tzu was angling in the river P'u, the king of Ch'u sent two high officers of state, who accosting Chuang Tzu announced that the king wished to entrust him with the management of all his domains. Rod in hand and eyes still fixed upon his line, Chuang Tzu replied, 'I have been told that in Ch'u there is a

holy tortoise that died three thousand years ago. The
king keeps it in the great hall of his ancestral shrine, in
a casket covered with a cloth. Suppose that when this
tortoise was caught, it had been allowed to choose
between dying and having its bones venerated for centuries to come or going on living with its tail draggling
in the mud, which would it have preferred?' 'No doubt,'
said the two officers, 'it would have preferred to go on
living with its tail draggling in the mud.' 'Well then, be
off with you,' said Chuang Tzu, 'and leave me to drag
my tail in the mud.'

PART TWO

POLITICS

Contemporary Events

Hitherto we have been journeying with Chuang Tzu 'in the realm of Nothing Whatever,' in territories of the mind where 'now and long ago are one.' But there is in the book which bears Chuang Tzu's name much which cannot be understood without reference to what was actually happening in China in the second half of the 4th century B.C.

What we know for certain about this period is surprisingly little. Anecdotes and imaginary discourses abound. They have been arbitrarily attached to a defective system of chronology, and the result, though it teems with contradictions and impossibilities, has been accepted as history. Recent research, checked by the evidence of a few contemporary inscriptions, has however succeeded in establishing a meagre outline of fact, which I shall try to indicate here as simply and briefly as possible.

About the middle of the 4th century B.C. China was divided into a number of independent States. It is best to begin with Wei, because it lay in the centre of the group and also because we possess (in a mutilated form) a contemporary chronicle of this State which covers the whole period in question, whereas with regard to other States our information is much less reliable. From 365 B.C. onwards Wei had its capital near the modern K'ai-fêng Fu in Honan. To the west lay Ch'in, a land of fierce warriors, regarded by the Chinese as semi-barbarians, and certainly little affected as yet by the literary culture that had been built up far away, in eastern China. To the south lay Ch'u, a land with a literature and culture of its own. Chuang Tzu was not actually a man of Ch'u. But his native State Sung stood in close relationship with Ch'u, and parallels between Chuang Tzu and the works of the great Ch'u poet, Ch'ü Yüan, have often been pointed out.

To the east lay the kingdom of Ch'i, famous at this time for its patronage of philosophers. On the southern borders of Ch'i lay Lu, the home of Confucius. It is seldom mentioned in the records of the period and had completely lost its political importance. To the north lay the kingdoms of Yen (the modern Peking) and Chao, in constant warfare with the horse-nomads of the Mongolian steppe, from whom they learnt and transmitted to the rest of China the art of fighting on horseback and many of the cultural elements that happened to be associated with it; such as the use of gold ornaments.

The main process that we can see at work during the whole period is the gradual expansion in every direction of the Ch'in State, leading up to the complete unification of China under Ch'in rule in 221 B.C. Looking at events from the centre outwards, that is to say, from the point of view of Wei, we find Prince Hui of Wei, who ascended the throne in 368 B.C., pursuing a policy of defence and internal consolidation. In 361 he drained the P'u-t'ien swamps which lay to the west of his Capital; in 359 he built a Great Wall to defend his western frontier. The period between 361 and 355 is presumably the Seven Years' Peace referred to by Chuang Tzu in a passage about to be quoted.

But in 354 the eastern frontier of Wei was violated by the Ch'i, and in a great battle at Kueiyang in southern Shantung the armies of Wei were defeated and put to flight.

Ten years later Wei was again defeated by Ch'i, this time at Ma-ling in southern Hopei; the Crown Prince of Wei was captured and apparently died in captivity, for the king of Wei said to Mencius:[1] 'On the east we were defeated by Ch'i and my eldest son died there.'

Three hundred and forty-two B.C. was a particularly bad year for Wei. In the summer the eastern frontier was invaded by Ch'i and Sung; in the autumn the famous Shang Tzu (regarded as the founder of Ch'in's greatness) led his armies into Wei from the west, and two months later Chao attacked Wei from the north. In this year the supremacy of Ch'in as leader among the States was formally acknowledged by the other rulers of China.

South of the Yangtze River lay two ancient maritime States that had only partially adopted Chinese culture: Wu, centring round what is now Suchow, and Yüeh, centring round what is now Ningpo. Long ago, in 473 B.C., Yüeh had swallowed up Wu. Now it was the turn of Yüeh to dwindle. In 333 the great southern State of Ch'u defeated and killed the king of Yüeh, and annexed the old Wu territory.

During the next few years Ch'in was continually

[1] Mencius, Legge, p. 10.

driving the Wei eastwards, by a series of encroachments which it is difficult to chronologize exactly.
But Ch'in was not only expanding to the east. The
barbarians (Jung) of Kansu were also being subjected; in 327 B.C. the I-ch'ü, who astonished the
Chinese by burning instead of burying their dead,
became subject to Ch'in. In 323 Wei, already har-
assed on east and west, began also to be threatened
in the south. 'In the south we have been humiliated
by Ch'u,' says the king of Wei in the passage already
quoted from *Mencius*, referring almost certainly to
the battle of Hsiang-ling (eastern Honan). In 322–
320 the Ch'in were already south of the Yellow River,
perilously near to the Wei Capital; in 316, again
moving south, they annexed the semi-barbarian State
of Shu, in what is now Szechuan. About this time
internal troubles broke out in the northern State
of Yen. Ch'i 'came to the rescue,' marched unop-
posed into Yen, and one morning the people of Yen
woke up to discover that Yen no longer existed; it
was part of Greater Ch'i. This was in 314. Before
the end of the year the people of Yen grew tired of
their saviours and revolted.

But to return to Wei; in 313 the Ch'in again
crossed the Yellow River and captured Chiao in
western Honan, and after prolonged struggles, interrupted perhaps by a civil war in Ch'in, in 290 Wei
surrendered the greater part of its Shansi territory
to Ch'in.

There was what we should call a Collective Security school[1] which believed that Ch'in intended to
'swallow up everything under Heaven,' and looked

---

[1] It is certain that these ways of thought actually existed;
but the speeches in which they are dramatized in the
Chan Kuo Ts'ê are imaginary.

upon a defensive alliance of the other States and the isolation of Ch'in as the only chance of safety. Other incidental advantages of close relationship between the great northern and southern States were held out as a bait. For example, a protagonist of this policy assured king Wei of Ch'u (died, 329 B.C.) that it would lead to his 'harem being full of lovely girls skilled in music, his stables being full of horses and camels' from the northern lands. The men of Ch'in were represented as veritable 'tigers and wolves' with whom it was immoral to have any relationship.

On the other hand there was a pro-Ch'in school which hoped that the ambitions of Ch'in would be satisfied by a limited expansion eastwards and southwards, and refused to believe that a State so large as Ch'u or one so densely populated and prosperous as Ch'i was in any real danger. The leader of the pro-Ch'in school was Chang I, who died in 310 B.C. In 313 we find him demanding that Ch'u should close her north-eastern frontier and break off the alliance with Ch'i, in return for which he offered the king of Ch'u 600 leagues of territory at Shang-yü (in south-western Honan) and girls from Ch'in 'who shall be your concubines, Great King, and wait upon you hand and foot.' The king of Ch'u accordingly broke with Ch'i. Meanwhile Chang I, pretending to have had an accident when mounting his chariot, absented himself from Court for three months after his return to Ch'in. The Ch'in government affected to know nothing about the bargain with Ch'u; no concubines arrived, no territory was ceded. The king of Ch'u, realizing that he had been tricked, made a desperate attempt to renew relations with Ch'i, his messenger crossing the frontier with

a borrowed Sung passport. He arrived too late; Ch'i
had already allied itself with Ch'in.

When the powerful and aggressive State of Ch'in
was threatening destruction to the other States of
China, the rhetorician Shun-yü K'un went to the
ruler of Wei and advocated an alliance of the other
States against Ch'in. The ruler of Wei was so much
impressed by his arguments that he at once des-
patched Shun-yü K'un to the neighbouring State of
Ch'u, to negotiate an alliance. But fearing that his
reputation as a rhetorician would suffer if it were
thought that he could only argue on one side, Shun-
yü K'un returned to Court just when the mission
was about to start and made an equally impressive
speech in favour of an understanding with Ch'in.
The result was that the mission to Ch'u was counter-
manded; but the ruler of Wei could not bring himself to adopt the alternative policy of an understanding with the 'wolves of Ch'in,' and Shun-yü K'un
was no longer admitted to the Court.[1]

What was the attitude of the Taoist towards all
these marches and counter-marches, bargains and
ruses, towards the reckless slaughter and destruction
that had been devastating China for a hundred
years? Like all Taoist attitudes it is better illustrated
by a fable than by a disquisition:

'There is a creature,' said Tai Chin Jên to the king of
Wei, 'that is called the bull-frog. Has your Majesty ever
heard of it?' 'Indeed I have,' said the king of Wei. 'On
the bull-frog's left horn,' said Tai Chin Jên, 'is a country
called Buffet; on its right horn is a country called Maul.
These two countries have never been able to decide
where Maul ends and Buffet begins. Over the question

[1] *Huai-nan Tzu*, XII.

of this disputed territory battle after battle is fought; the corpses lie piled in their tens of thousands, and even when one side or the other has been dislodged from the disputed ground, the victors are not content to go quietly home, but pursue and harry the retreating foe for weeks on end.' 'What futile nonsense!' said the king indignantly. 'Pray allow me to show you,' said Tai Chin Jên, 'that my story, so far from being nonsense, is very much to the point indeed. Do you, my lord, believe that space is limited, or that it stretches on for ever above and below, north, south, east and west?' 'There is no limit to it,' said the king. 'So then, to someone who knew how to make his mind travel into the illimitable, the "lands that are in communication" would seem a mere insignificant speck?' 'Yes,' said the king. 'Among these lands that are in communication,' said Tai Chin Jên, 'is Wei. In Wei is the city of Ta Liang, and in that city is your Majesty. Are you really so different from the king of Maul?' 'Not very different,' said the king.

The objection of the Taoist to war is not based on moral or humanitarian grounds. 'To love the people is to harm them; to side with those who are in the right in order to end war is the way to start fresh wars.' It is based on the absolute insignificance and futility of the utmost that conquest can gain or that defence can secure, when compared with the limitless inward resources of the individual. 'What am I to do?' asked the same king of Wei, when his Commander-in-Chief[1] pleaded for war with Ch'i and his minister told him that the Commander-

[1] Kung-sun Yen. 'Give me two hundred thousand armed men,' said this amiable generalissimo, 'and I will capture all their people, carry off their horses and cattle, deal with their king in a way that will considerably cool his ardour, and then take his city. I will pursue their general and lash his back till I break his spine.'

in-Chief was a scoundrel. 'It is quite true,' said the Taoist Hua Tzu, 'that those who advise you to attack Ch'i are scoundrels; and equally true that those who plead so eloquently for peace with Ch'i are also scoundrels. And anyone who stopped short at telling you that both were scoundrels would himself be a scoundrel too.' 'What then am I to do?' said the king. 'Seek Tao,' said Hua Tzu, 'that is all you need do.'

The Uncarved Block

P'u means wood in its natural condition, uncarved and unpainted. It is the Taoist symbol of man's natural state, when his inborn powers (tê) have not been tampered with by knowledge or circumscribed by morality. The Taoist cult of p'u is a philosophic restatement of ancient ritual ideas: 'If thou wilt make me an altar of stone thou shalt not build it of hewn stone: for if thou lift up thy tool upon it, thou hast polluted it.'[1] The enemies of this simplicity are the sense-organs, with their separate and limited functions. 'The eye is a menace to clear sight, the ear is a menace to subtle hearing, the mind is a menace to wisdom, every organ of the senses is a menace to its own capacity. Sad is it indeed that man should look upon these seats of menace as his greatest treasure.'

What then is man's true treasure? It is his Inward Vision (ming), a generalized perception that can come into play only when the distinction between

[1] Exodus xx. 25.

'inside' and 'outside,' between 'self' and 'things,'
between 'this' and 'that' has been entirely oblit-
erated. Chuang Tzu's symbol for this state of pure
consciousness, which sees without looking, hears
without listening, knows without thinking, is the
god Hun-tun ('Chaos'): 'Fuss, the god of the Southern Ocean, and Fret, the god of the Northern Ocean,
happened once to meet in the realm of Chaos, the
god of the centre. Chaos treated them very hand-
somely and they discussed together what they could
do to repay his kindness. They had noticed that,
whereas everyone else has seven apertures, for sight,
hearing, eating, breathing and so on, Chaos had
none. So they decided to make the experiment of
boring holes in him. Every day they bored a hole,
and on the seventh day Chaos died.'

Just as the Taoist cult of p'u, the uncarved Block,
is founded on ancient ritual ideas, so too this fable
is no doubt an adaptation of a very ancient myth.
We can indeed get some idea of the sort of primitive
myth which Chuang Tzu is here refining and inter-
preting by comparing the story of Hun-tun (Chaos)
with the Australian myth of Anjir: 'In the beginning
Anjir was lying in the shadow of a thickly-leaved
tree. He was a black-fellow with very large buttocks,
but peculiar in that there was no sign of any orifice.
Yalpan happened to be passing by at the time and
noticing this anomaly made a cut in the usual place
by means of a piece of quartz-crystal.'[1] Approaching
the myth of Hun-tun from a quite different point of
view, M. Granet[2] regards it as an 'échange de presta-
tions'; 'une opération chirurgicale mythique com-

[1] M. F. Ashley-Montagu, *Coming into Being among the
Australian Aborigines*, p. 130.
[2] *Danses et Légendes*, p. 544.

pense une bonne réception.' This strange interpretation reads like a parody of what is called the 'sociological approach,' a method which M. Granet has himself often turned to such good account.

The Golden Age

To the question, 'What would happen if everyone turned Taoist, how could a community exist at all, if all the minds in it were "wandering in the Illimitable?"' the Taoist answer would again be, 'Seek Tao yourself; that is all you need to do.' But there are passages in Chuang Tzu and other Taoist books where an ideal State is depicted, the sort of community in which the Taoist would have liked to find himself. There are no books; the people have no use for any form of record save knotted ropes. 'They relish the simplest sorts of food, have no desire for fine clothing, take pleasure in their rustic tasks, are content to remain in their homes. The next village might be so close that one could hear the cocks crowing in it, the dogs barking, but the people would grow old and die without ever having been there.'

The people in the Golden Age here described have dogs and chickens, and know how to make ropes. We must suppose that they lived by agriculture which some Taoists regarded as man's 'natural' occupation: 'When the people are allowed to do what is ordinary and natural to them, they wear the clothes that they have woven and eat the food that they have grown.'[1] But though this, rather than

[1] IX. b.

the life of court and camp, is the natural life of men as they exist today, there was in the beginning, in the time of the primeval Chaos (*hun-mang*), a state of absolute harmony between man and his surroundings, a life as effortless and spontaneous as the passage of the seasons: the two vital principles of Yin and Yang worked together instead of in opposition. 'Ghosts and spirits molested no one, the weather was perfect, the ten thousand things were unblemished, no living creature died before its time . . . no one did anything, but everything always happened of itself.'

Then came the culture-heroes, inventors of fire, house-building, agriculture and the like.

The Taoists objected to machinery. There are of course many grounds upon which labour-saving devices may be condemned. The common modern objection is that they cause unemployment; but religious leaders (Gandhi, for example) reject them on the ground that they have a degrading effect on those who use them. The Taoist objection was of of the latter kind:

Tzu-kung, the disciple of Confucius, after travelling to Ch'u in the south, came back by way of Chin. When he was passing through Han-yin he saw an old man who was engaged in irrigating his vegetable plots. The way this old man did it was to let himself down into the well-pit by footholes cut in the side and emerge clasping a pitcher which he carefully emptied into a channel, thus expending a great deal of energy with very small results.

'There exists,' Tzu-kung said to him, 'a contrivance with which one can irrigate a hundred vegetable plots in a single day. Unlike what you are doing, it demands a very small expenditure of energy, but produces very great results. Would you not like me to tell you about it?' The gardener raised his head and gazed at Tzu-kung. 'What is it like?' he asked. 'It is an instrument carved out of wood,' said Tzu-kung, 'heavy behind and light in front. It scoops up the water like a bale, as quickly as one drains a bath-tub. Its name is the well-sweep.' A look of indignation came into the gardener's face. He laughed scornfully, saying, 'I used to be told by my teacher that where there are cunning contrivances there will be cunning performances, and where there are cunning performances there will be cunning hearts. He in whose breast a cunning heart lies has blurred the pristine purity of his nature; he who has blurred the pristine purity of his nature has troubled the quiet of his soul, and with one who has troubled the quiet of his soul Tao will not dwell. It is not that I do not know about this invention; but that I should be ashamed to use it.'

We must then 'bind the fingers' of the technicians, 'smash their arcs and plumb-lines, throw away their compasses and squares.' Only then will men learn to rely on their inborn skill, on the 'Great Skill that looks like clumsiness.' But the culture-heroes were not the only inventors who 'tampered with men's hearts.' Equally pernicious (as will be seen in the next section) were on the one hand the Sages, inventors of goodness and duty, and of the laws which enforce an artificial morality; and on the other, the tyrants, inventors of tortures and inquisitions, 'embitterers of man's nature.'

Government

Only a king who can forget his kingdom should be entrusted with a kingdom. So long as he is 'wandering alone with Tao' all will be 'peace, quietness, and security.' But his subjects will not know why this is so; it will seem to them that 'it happened of its own accord.' Nor will the king know himself to be the saviour of men and things; he 'seeks Tao; that is all.'

One that is born beautiful, even if you give him a mirror, unless you tell him so will not know that he is more beautiful than other men. But the fact that he knows it or does not know it, is told about it or is not told about it, makes no difference at all to the pleasure that others get from his beauty or to the admiration that it arouses. Beauty is his nature. And so it is with the love of the Sage for his people. Even if they give him fame, unless someone tells him, he will not know that he loves his people. But the fact that he knows it or does not know it, is told of it or is not told of it, makes no difference at all either to his love for the people or the peace that this love brings to them. Love is his nature.

Ts'ui Chü said to Lao Tzu, 'You say there must be no government. But if there is no government, how are men's hearts to be improved?' 'The last thing you should do,' said Lao Tzu, 'is to tamper with men's hearts. The heart of man is like a spring; if you press it down, it only springs up the higher. . . . It can be hot as the fiercest fire; cold as the hardest ice. So swift is it that in the space of a nod it can go twice to the end of the world and back again. In repose, it is quiet as the bed of a pool; in action, mysterious as Heaven. A wild steed that cannot be tethered—such is the heart of man.'

The first to tamper with men's hearts was the Yellow Ancestor,[1] when he taught goodness and duty. The Sages Yao and Shun in obedience to his teaching slaved till 'there was no hair on their shanks, no down on their

[1] Yellow Emperor is the usual translation.

thighs' to nourish the bodies of their people, wore out
their guts by ceaseless acts of goodness and duty, exhausted their energies by framing endless statutes and
laws. Yet all this was not enough to make the people
good. Yao had to banish Huan Tou to Mount Ch'ung,
drive the San Miao to the desert of San Wei, exile
Kung-kung in the Land of the North—things which he
would not have had to do if he had been equal to his
task. In the ages that followed bad went to worse. The
world saw on the one hand the tyrant Chieh and the
brigand Chih; on the other, the virtuous Master Tsêng[1]
and the incorruptible Shih Yü. There arose at last the
schools of Confucius and Mo Tzu.[2] Henceforward the
pleased and the angry began to suspect one another, the
foolish and the wise to despise one another, the good
and the bad to disappoint one another, charlatans and
honest men to abuse one another. Decay set in on every
hand. Men's natural powers no longer came into play;
their inborn faculties were wholly corrupted. Everywhere it was knowledge that was admired and the common people became knowing and sly.

Henceforward nothing was left in its natural state. It
must be hacked and sawed into some new shape, slit
just where the inked line had marked it, broken up with
hammer and chisel, till the whole world was in utter
chaos and confusion. All this came from tampering with
the heart of man!

Those who saw the folly of such methods fled to the
mountains and hid in inaccessible caves; the lords of ten
thousand chariots sat quaking in their ancestral halls.
Today, when those that fell by the executioner's hand
lie pillowed corpse on corpse, when prisoners bowed
down beneath the cangue are driven on in such flocks
that they have scarcely room to pass, when the maimed
and mutilated jostle one another in their throngs, the

[1] Disciple of Confucius.
[2] See below, p. 121.

Confucians and the followers of Mo Tzu can find nothing better to do, amid the shackled and gyved, than
straddle their legs, bare their arms and go for one another
as hard as they can. Is it believable that such impudence,
such shamelessness can exist? Almost I could fancy that
saintliness and wisdom were the clasp and catch that
fastened the prisoner's cangue; that goodness and duty
were the bolt and eye that fastened his gyves. Yes,
almost I could believe that Tsêng and Shih were the
whistling arrows that heralded the coming of brigand
Chih and tyrant Chieh.

When Po Chü came to Ch'i, he saw the body of a
malefactor, drawn and quartered. Binding together the
severed limbs, as one wraps a child in its swaddling-
clothes, he took off his Court dress, covered him with
it, cried aloud and lamented, saying, 'Oh, Sir, do not
think that you will be alone in your fate. Universal is
the disaster that has befallen you, though it has touched
you sooner than the rest. They say "Do not murder, do
not steal." But it was they who set some on high,
dragged down others to ignominy, putting before men's
eyes what drives them to discontent. It was they who
heaped up goods and possessions, putting before men's
eyes what drives them to strife. Set up what drives a
man to discontent, heap up what leads him to strife,
weary his limbs with toil, not giving him day in day out
a moment's rest, and what else can happen but that he
should end like this?'

The 'no-government' doctrine of the beginning of
this and similar passages in other Taoist books has
often been compared with the modern anarchism
of writers like Kropotkin. But there are important
differences. The modern anarchists regard government and religious morality as devices invented by
a privileged class in order to maintain its privileges;
whereas Taoism looks upon the Sages as misguided

altruists. Moreover, one of the main tenets of modern anarchism is that no appeal must be made to the authority of 'metaphysical entities'; and it can hardly be denied that, whatever else it may be or may not be, Tao is undoubtedly a 'metaphysical entity.'

But anarchists and Taoists are in agreement upon one fundamental point: laws produce criminals; eliminate the Sages who produce laws, and 'there will be peace and order everywhere under Heaven.'

Once a follower of the great brigand Chih asked him whether thieves had any use for wisdom and morality. 'To be sure, they do,' said the brigand Chih, 'just as much as other people. To find oneself in a strange house and guess unerringly where its treasures lie hid, this surely needs Inspiration. To be the first to enter needs Courage; to be the last to leave needs Sense of Duty. Never to attempt the impossible needs Wisdom. To divide the spoil fairly needs Goodness. Never has there been or could there be anyone who lacked these five virtues and yet became a really great brigand.' . . .[1] Thus no great brigand existed till the Sages who taught these virtues came into the world. If we thrashed the Sages and let the brigands and assassins go, there would soon be peace and order everywhere under Heaven.

Knowing that there are dishonest people who pry into boxes, delve in sacks, raise the lids of chests, to protect their property householders provide strong ropes and solid locks; and in the common opinion of the world they act wisely in doing so. But suppose real brigands come. They will snatch up the boxes, hoist the sacks, carry away the big trunks on their backs, and be gone; only too glad that the locks are solid and the

[1] This story of 'honour among thieves' exists in many varying forms, for example in *Lü Shih Ch'un Ch'iu*, 54, *Huai-nan Tzu*, XII. 37, *Pao P'u Tzu*, XII.

ropes strong. The sole result of what before seemed wisdom was that the brigands were saved the trouble of packing.

Now I would go so far as to maintain that everything commonly regarded as wisdom is simply 'packing for brigands,' and everything that is commonly regarded as saintliness is simply 'storing loot for brigands.' How do I know that this is so? Throughout the whole length and breadth of the land of Ch'i (a territory so populous that in any village the sound of the cocks crowing and the dogs barking in the next village could be plainly heard), wherever net or snare was spread, wherever rake or ploughshare cleft the soil, within the four frontiers of all this great territory two thousand leagues square, not a shrine was set up, not a Holy Ground or Sheaf, not a rule was made in village or household, county or district, province or quarter, that did not tally with the ordinances of the Saviour Kings of old. Yet within the space of a single day T'ien Ch'êng Tzu slew the prince of Ch'i[1] and stole his kingdom. And not his kingdom only, but with it all the laws and policies of the Sages and wise men by which the princes of Ch'i had ruled their land. True, T'ien Ch'êng Tzu is known to history as a robber and assassin; but in his day he dwelt secure as any Yao or Shun. The small States dared not reprove him; the great States dared not punish him, and for twelve generations his descendants have held the land of Ch'i . . .

Dealing with the World

The Taoist does not 'hide himself away in the woods and hills.' What he hides is not his body, but his *tê*, his inborn powers. He knows how to 'follow others

[1] In 481 B.C.

without losing his Self.' And for this reason the art of the courtier, to which so much space is devoted by other writers of the third century, is not ignored by Taoist literature.

When Yen Ho was about to take up his duties as tutor to the heir of Ling Duke of Wei, he went to Ch'ü Po Yü for advice. 'I have to deal,' he said, 'with a man of depraved and murderous disposition. If I do not hinder him in his crimes, I shall be endangering my country; if I do hinder him, I shall endanger my own life. Such shrewdness as he has consists entirely in recognizing other people's shortcomings; it fails entirely to apprise him of his own. How is one to deal with a man of this sort?' 'I am glad,' said Ch'ü Po Yü, 'that you have asked this question. You will need much caution and care. The first thing you must do is not to improve him, but to improve yourself. It is essential that your outward conduct should be accommodating, and equally essential that your heart should be at peace. And yet, both these essentials have their danger. The outward accommodation must on no account affect what is within; nor must the peace that is within betray itself outside. For if what should be outward goes below the surface,

> "You will stumble, you will stagger,
> You will topple and expire."

Whereas if the inward peace of the heart betrays itself on the surface,

> "Comes recognition, comes fame,
> Comes bale and woe."

If the person of whom you speak behaves like a baby, you too must behave like a baby. If he has his foibles, you too must have your foibles. If he behaves like a cad, then you too must behave like a cad. And if you probe[1]

[1] Perform acupuncture; of course meant metaphorically.

him, do so in a part where his skin is not sore. Do you not know the story of the mantis in the wheel-rut, how it tried to stop the chariot by waving its arms, and did not realize that, useful though they had always proved, this was a task beyond what they could accomplish? The mantis's arms are the part upon which it has most right to pride itself. Be very careful not to meet a bad man's villainy by displaying to him what is best in you. For that way danger lies. Have you not heard how a keeper of beasts deals with his tigers? He never ventures to give them a live creature to eat, because when they have killed they become fierce. He never gives them a whole animal to eat, because when they rend flesh they become savage. He knows that what can be done with them when they are sated cannot be done when they are hungry. Tigers and men, though so different in species, have this at least in common: towards those that look after them their feelings will be friendly so long as they are humoured; and if despite what is done for them they turn savage, it is because their moods have not been studied.

'There was a man who dearly loved his horse. He carried away its droppings in a basket; he scooped up its stale in a clam-shell. One day a fly attached itself to the animal, and this man scotched it. Taken by surprise the horse began to plunge and rear, broke its halter, bruised its head, tore its breast. His intentions were for the creature's good; but it was his affection for it that proved the cause of its undoing. This should be a warning to you.'

But there is an art of 'living in the world' (the Buchmanites seem also to have discovered it) which might perhaps be better defined as living on the world. It is practised by the 'Man of Té,' whose inward powers are so highly developed that the outward sources of his well-being are entirely unknown to him: 'Whether at home or abroad, he takes no thought for the future; he is free alike from approval and disapproval, from admiration and disgust. . . . He seems as bewildered as an infant that has lost its mother, as helpless as a traveller who has lost his way; yet, though he has no idea where they come from, he is amply provided with all the goods and chattels a man can need; and though he does not know how they got there, he has always plenty of drink and food. Such is the description of the Man of Tê.'

I will close the section on Chuang Tzu with a story which has a certain current interest, for it was quoted at the Treasury by the representatives of the Chinese Government who came to England to raise a loan in 1938. The representatives of the Treasury (or so I was told by a Chinese friend) said they could not see that it was relevant:

Once Chuang Tzu was reduced to such extremities that he was faced with starvation and was obliged to go to the prince of Wei and ask for some millet. 'I am hoping before long,' said the prince of Wei, 'to receive the rent-money from the tenants in my fief. Then I shall be pleased to lend you three hundred pieces; will that be all right?' 'On my way here yesterday,' said Chuang Tzu, looking very indignant, 'I suddenly heard a voice somewhere in the roadway calling for help. I looked round, and there in the cart-track was a gudgeon. "Gudgeon," I said, "what are you doing there?" "I am an exile from the eastern seas," said the gudgeon. "Let me have a peck-measure of water, and you will save my life." "I am hoping before long," I said to it, "to go south to Wu and Yüeh. I will ask the king to dam the western river, so that it may flow your way. Will that be all right?" "I have lost my proper surroundings and have no place to call my own," said the gudgeon. "All the same, if you gave me a peck-measure of water I could manage to keep alive. If instead of that you do what you propose, you might as well string me up at once in the dried-fish shop." '

Mencius

The Better Feelings

The whole teaching of Mencius centres round the word Goodness (jên). Different schools of Confucianism meant different things by this term. But to Mencius, Goodness meant compassion; it meant not being able to bear that others should suffer. It meant a feeling of responsibility for the sufferings of others, such as was felt by the legendary Yü, subduer of the primeval Flood: 'If anyone were drowned, Yü felt as though it were he himself that had drowned him.' Or such as was felt (so it was said) in ancient times by the counsellor I Yin to whom if he knew that a single man or woman anywhere under Heaven were not enjoying the benefits of wise rule, 'it was as though he had pushed them into a ditch with his own hand; so heavy was the responsibility that he put upon himself for everything that happened under Heaven.'

According to Mencius, feelings such as this are not produced by education. They are the natural birthright of everyone, they are his 'good capacity,' his 'good knowledge,' his 'good feelings,' and the problem of education is not how to get them, but how to keep them. 'He who lets these feelings go and does not know how to recover them is to be pitied indeed! If anyone has a chicken or dog that has strayed, he takes steps to recover them; but people are content to let their good feelings go and make no effort to find them again. Yet what else is education but the recovery of good feelings that have strayed away?' How these feelings are lost, how they are rubbed away by the rough contacts of daily life, is described by Mencius in the allegory of the Bull Mountain:

The Bull Mountain was once covered with lovely trees. But it is near the capital of a great State. People came with their axes and choppers; they cut the woods down, and the mountain has lost its beauty. Yet even so, the day air and the night air came to it, rain and dew moistened it till here and there fresh sprouts began to grow. But soon cattle and sheep came along and browsed on them, and in the end the mountain became gaunt and bare, as it is now. And seeing it thus gaunt and bare people imagine that it was woodless from the start. Now just as the natural state of the mountain was quite different from what now appears, so too in every man (little though they may be apparent) there assuredly were once feelings of decency and kindness; and if these good feelings are no longer there, it is that they have been tampered with, hewn down with axe and bill. As each day dawns they are assailed anew. What chance then has our nature, any more than that mountain, of keeping its beauty? To us, too, comes the air of day, the air of night. Just at dawn, indeed, we have for a moment and in a certain degree a mood in which our promptings and aversions come near to being such as are proper to men. But something is sure to happen before the morning is over, by which these better feelings are ruffled or destroyed. And in the end, when they have been ruffled again and again, the night air is no longer able to preserve them, and soon our feelings are as near as may be to those of beasts and birds; so that anyone might make the same mistake about us as about the mountain, and think that there was never any good in us from the very start. Yet assuredly our present state of feeling is not what we begin with. Truly,

> 'If rightly tended, no creature but thrives;
> If left untended, no creature but pines away.'

Confucius said:

> 'Hold fast to it and you can keep it,
> Let go, and it will stray.
> For its comings and goings it has no time nor
> tide;
> None knows where it will bide.'

Surely it was of the feelings[1] that he was speaking.

How, then, can our 'good feelings,' at their height in the calm of dawn, be protected against the inroads of daily agitation? Naturally, by controlled breathing. The passage in which Mencius discusses his breath-technique is hopelessly corrupt and obscure. But that deep and regular breathing calms and fortifies the mind is a matter of common experience. That a definite technique of breath-control, practised over long periods, can reach a point at which ordinary consciousness is voluntarily suspended, would not be denied by anyone familiar with Zen or with Indian yoga. But how far Mencius went in yoga technique, what exactly was the nature of his 'flood breath,' *hao-jan chih ch'i*, it is impossible to say. He himself, when asked what the phrase meant, replied: 'It is difficult to say.' As it was capable of 'filling everything between Heaven and Earth' it was clearly envisaged as something supra-normal, something more than the air that goes in and out of the lungs. Yet it is wrong to call it spirit, energy, passion or the like; for none of these words include the idea of

[1] The innate good feelings.

'breath,' whereas Mencius's *ch'i*, whatever else it may be besides, is first and foremost 'breath.'

Government by Goodness

Goodness, as we have seen, depends on peace of mind, and Mencius realized that this again depends on economic security. 'If beans and millet were as plentiful as fire and water, such a thing as a bad man would not exist among the people.' Consequently the various (and partly identical) discourses of Mencius about Government by Goodness, supposed to have been addressed to the rulers of Wei, Ch'i and T'êng, consist largely of advice about land tenure, taxation and what we should call Old Age Pensions (*yang lao*, 'nourishing the aged').

The views of Mencius on land tenure, at any rate in the form in which they have reached us, are hardly less obscure than his views on breath-technique. In traditional theory, all land belonged to the Emperor. In practice, as the Emperor existed only in name, it belonged to the rulers of the various States, who retained a great deal of it themselves, and gave the use of the rest to nobles and gentlemen. Together with the right to use an estate went the right to employ the labour of the local peasants, who in return for a rent roughly amounting to a tenth of the produce of the estate—there were many variations of the system—had the right to the rest of the produce. Sometimes part of the estate was set aside as 'public land' and the whole of its produce went to the land-lord;[1] in such cases the whole produce of the rest

[1] Who was very often the ruler himself.

of the estate (the 'private land') went to the peasants. No doubt there were wide variations of custom, locally and at different periods. But this seems to be the general picture.

A recent writer has stated that Mencius wanted to change this system into an 'economic institution having socialistic implications.' 'The land is to be given by the State to the people, who cultivate it in a condition of liberty.' There is not a single passage in *Mencius* which supports such an interpretation. Evidently the traditional system, such as I have outlined, was no longer fully observed in the three States which Mencius desired to reform. It had been devised at a time when agriculture was shifting and 'predatory'; after one plot had been cultivated for several seasons and ceased to give a good yield, it was simply abandoned, and fresh land was cleared and brought under cultivation. But when, in areas where no free land was left, agriculture became settled and stationary, it became necessary to let each plot in turn lie fallow for several seasons. The system of rent must have required adjustment to this new state of affairs; the taxation or non-taxation of fallow land must have been the crux of the problem. But this question is never definitely referred to by Mencius.

Agriculture is of course necessarily a co-operative business. An individual cannot support himself by ploughing, sowing and reaping unaided. And if this is true of cereal crops (wheat, barley, and the like), it is even more obviously true of rice-culture, with its complicated processes of replanting and irrigation. While agriculture is still in the predatory stage, while new fields are constantly being wrested from jungle or prairie by burning and hewing, the need for collaboration not merely of a whole family or household but of larger groups is evident. It was commonly believed that in old days eight families had worked together, and Mencius wanted to revive this system of collaboration, at any rate in remoter country districts (where perhaps it had not fallen altogether into abeyance), and to encourage the general spirit of co-operation that went with it; 'the people make friends on their way to the fields and back again, they help one another in keeping watch and·ward, assist and support one another in times of sickness; and so everyone becomes intimate and friendly.'

Contrasted with this system and utterly condemned by Mencius was the *kung*, the tribute system, in which each householder had to pay a fixed tribute of grain, determined by the average yield of the land he tilled. This meant that in bad years people had to borrow grain at high rates of interest in order to pay the full tribute.

The obligations of the peasant did not end with the paying of rent on the lands that he cultivated. His labour was also conscripted for the building of palaces, treasuries, arsenals, city walls, and defences of all kinds; and he was of course liable at any time to be called away on military service. Moreover there were taxes on produce sold in the markets, frontier tariffs on imports from other States, vast enclosures in which all hunting rights were reserved for the ruler, and similar fishing reserves.

Government by Goodness meant the abolition of market taxes and frontier taxes; the reduction to a minimum of parks and enclosures; the use of conscripted labour only at times of the year when agriculture was slack. It meant the abolition of savage penalties; it meant public support for the aged; it meant schools in which the teaching centred on moral instruction. It is indeed a pity that Mencius tells us nothing about these schools save that they should exist; adding only some punning etymologies on the various names by which they had been known in the past.

Anyone who adopts these measures, even in a small State, will become a True King, that is to say, a monarch accepted by all China, dominating not by force but by goodness.

MENCIUS AND
THE KINGS

The Kings of Wei

 King Hui of Wei was an old man, probably getting on for seventy, when Mencius came to his Court. His long reign had been marked by disastrous wars,[1] in which his son had perished. His first question to Mencius was an unfortunate one. 'Sir,' he said, 'since you have thought it worth while to travel a thousand leagues to visit me, I feel sure that you have something to tell me which will be of profit to my kingdom.' To Mencius the word 'profit' represented expediency as opposed to right, worldliness as opposed

[1] See above, p. 60.

to morality. 'Why must your Majesty needs speak of profit?' he asked indignantly. 'All that I have to say to you is concerned with goodness and right, and with nothing else at all. If your Majesty asks "How can I profit my Kingdom?" your great officers will soon be asking "How can I profit my family?", your lesser officers and common subjects will be asking "How can I profit myself?" And while those above and those below are all scrambling for profit, your kingdom will fall into peril. . . . I would have your Majesty speak only of goodness and right. There is no need to bring in the word "profit." '

King Hui was a little better than some other kings. This was the most that Mencius was willing to concede:

'You must admit,' said the king, 'that I have taken a great deal of trouble about my kingdom. When the crops failed on the north side of the river, I moved the peasants across to the east side and sent grain to those who were left behind; and when the crops failed to the east of the river, I did the same thing. When I look round and see how neighbouring kingdoms are ruled, I do not find anyone who takes as much trouble as I do. Why is it that despite all this the population of neighbouring countries does not decrease, and our own does not increase?'

'Your Majesty,' answered Mencius, 'is fond of war, so let me take an illustration connected with soldiering. The drum sounds with a loud noise, weapons cross. Suddenly there is a panic, a lot of soldiers run away, throwing down their helmets and letting their weapons trail after them. Some run a hundred paces before they stop; some only fifty paces. Suppose those who stopped after fifty paces laughed at those who stopped after a hundred paces, what should you think?' 'They could not,' said the king. 'They may have run away less than a hundred paces, but they ran away all the same.' 'Since that is your view,' said Mencius, 'your Majesty must not expect an increase in the number of his subjects at the expense of neighbouring kingdoms.'

Hui died in 320 B.C. and was succeeded by King Hsiang, who had not even the merit of being 'a little better than the rest.' On coming out from his first interview with the new king, Mencius said to someone whom he met: 'The moment I set eyes upon him I could see that he looked quite unfit to be a ruler of men, and on closer contact I found him wholly lacking in dignity. He asked me abruptly "How could we get a world settlement?" "By unification," I said. "Who is capable of uniting the world?" he asked. "If there were a single ruler," I said, "who did not delight in slaughter, he could unite the whole world." "And who would side with him?" he asked. "Everyone in the world," I replied. "Your Majesty knows how in the seventh and eighth months the new grain becomes parched. But soon the clouds roll up, heavy rain falls, and the young plants shoot up in lusty growth. When this is so, it is as though nothing could hold them back. Today among those that are the shepherds of men there is not in the whole world one who does not delight in slaughter. Should such a one arise, then all people on earth would look towards him with outstretched necks. If he were indeed such a one, the people would come to him as water flows downward, in a flood that none could hold back." '

King Hsiang is not mentioned again, and it is commonly supposed that Mencius left Wei soon after his accession.

About King Hsiang Mencius had, as we have seen,

no illusions from the start. But with the accession of Prince Hung to the dukedom of T'êng, a small principality close to Mencius's birthplace, it seemed as though 'government by goodness' was at last going to have its trial. On a very small scale, indeed; for T'êng was only about ten miles square. But that did not matter; it was large enough to turn into a 'good kingdom'; and 'should a True King (*wang*) arise,' he would certainly come to T'êng to take notes about its ways, and thus a little dukedom would become 'a tutor of kings.'

The Duke of T'êng

The relations between Mencius and the duke of T'êng had begun before his accession. Business had taken him to Ch'u in the South and he had gone considerably out of his way in order to visit Mencius, who was then living in Sung. Mencius discoursed to him upon the fundamental goodness of human nature, frequently citing the careers of the legendary monarchs Yao and Shun. On his way back the prince again visited Mencius, who assured him that there was 'only one Way,' applicable alike to the smallest principality or the mightiest kingdom.

When the old duke died, duke Wên (as the prince had now become) said to his tutor Jan Yu, 'Some time ago when I was in Sung I had a conversation with Mencius, which I have never forgotten. And now that unfortunately the great calamity[1] has befallen me, I should like you to go to him, that I may

[1] The death of his father.

have his advice before I take in hand what must be done.'[1]

So Jan Yu went to Tsou and asked Mencius for his advice. 'This is splendid!' said Mencius. 'The proper discharge of funeral duties towards a parent taxes a man to his utmost. . . . The rites to be practised in the case of a ruler I have never studied. However, I have heard it said that the three years mourning, with wearing of mourning robes of coarse cloth, and the eating of gruel, thick and thin—these are common to all, from the Son of Heaven downwards, and did not differ in any of the three dynasties.'

The duke accordingly embarked upon the 'three years mourning' as prescribed. But his ministers and the older members of his family were not at all in favour of it. 'None of the dukes of Lu, of whose family we are a cadet branch, ever carried out this "three years mourning," ' they protested. 'Nor did any of our own dukes in T'êng. It is not possible for you suddenly to revoke their institutions. Moreover it is written in the Records: In mourning and sacrifice the ancestors are to be followed.'

'I got it from someone,' said the duke, meaning that he had not simply invented the ritual out of his head, and he said to Jan Yu, 'In old days I am afraid I did not pay much attention to my studies and was more interested in driving and fencing. The consequence is that my uncles and the ministers do not think me capable of deciding a matter like this. I should be very sorry if I were not able to carry out this solemn duty as I wish. I want you to go to Mencius and ask him what I should do.'

'It is only by ignoring their protests,' said Mencius, 'that he can win them over. . . . What the superior

[1] With regard to the rites of mourning.

approves of, the inferior will end by approving even more than he. The gentleman's part is like that of the wind; the smaller man's part is like that of the grass. When the wind passes over it, the grass cannot choose but bend. This matter rests entirely in the prince's hands.'

When the tutor came back with this message, the prince said, 'It is quite true; it is really for me to decide.'

For five months he lived in a mourner's hut, without issuing instructions or admonitions of any kind. His ministers and relatives were much impressed, saying that he evidently understood these matters. When the time for the interment arrived, people came from far and wide to witness it. The sadness of his expression and the bitterness of his weeping and wailing gave great satisfaction to all who had come to condole with him.

The Three Years Mourning

The 'three years mourning' was one of the main tenets of the Confucian movement (until it became a State religion in Han times Confucianism was what we should call a 'movement,' in the sense in which the Chinese speak today of the New Life Movement, rather than a philosophic school). Naturally the Confucians represented it as a primeval institution, neglected only in a late and degenerate age. Their opponents, as in the passage above, decried it as an arbitrary innovation. In its full form the three years mourning (in reality it lasted twenty-five months, but it was so called because it extended into the third year) involved living in a shed near the tomb of the deceased, abstaining from sexual intercourse, wine, meat, music and visits to friends, and the maintenance, during the whole period, of an air of extreme dejection and decrepitude. Theoretically it followed the death of either parent, but in practice it was seldom carried out in its entirety in the case of the mother.

It is clear that such a practice must have represented not only an extreme disruption of family and social life, but also a great hindrance to bureaucratic efficiency. For any official whose father died was obliged immediately to quit office for over two years; there are instances, too, of office being quitted for one year upon the death of a grandfather or brother. The mourning for a wife, on the other hand, was a very short and mild affair. The ancestors of Confucius came from Sung. The Sung people were the descendants of the Shang, who were conquered, as tradition says, in the 12th century B.C. by the Chou. It has been recently suggested in China that Confucianism was, in its essence, a revival of Shang ideas, and the three years mourning with all its hampering and unpractical concomitants was originally a Shang institution.

It is true that one Shang king is said to have lived in the mourner's hovel and remained silent for three years,[1] and that nothing of this sort is related of any Chou king. Another Shang king is said, much against his will and only at the instigation of a wise minister, to have 'grieved' (not 'mourned' in any technical

[1] *Shu Ching*, Wu I.

sense) for three years;[1] but the source is a forgery of
the 3rd century A.D. In any case the whole complex
of Confucian reforms must be studied in its entirety.
The Confucians demanded not only an exaggerated
cult of dead parents but an extreme subservience to
parents while alive.[2] They insisted at the same time
upon a segregation of the sexes far stricter (as is
evident from numerous anecdotes of the preceding
centuries) than had hitherto been customary. These
demands seem to hang together psychologically, and
apart from the question of surviving Shang influence
(a possibility which I do not deny), they should be
studied in connexion with the whole process of social
disintegration which followed the break-up of the
early Chou empire.

Meanwhile, it is obvious that so inconvenient an
institution, whatever its psychological or historical
causes, would not have survived for centuries unless
it had some kind of concrete social value. In the life
of the official classes it certainly had such a value.
It represented a sort of 'sabbatical' occurring as a rule
towards the middle of a man's official career.[3] It gave

[1] *Shu Ching.* T'ai-chia. Earlier sources merely say that
on his succession the new king turned out 'not to be
clever' and was sent for three years to a country palace
to be coached.

[2] Those who wish to derive 'filial piety' from Shang institutions can find no better proof than certain vague
illusions, from the middle of the 3rd century B.C. onwards, to a Shang prince called Hsiao-chi who is supposed, from the contexts in which he is mentioned, to
have shown filial piety towards his father, but not to
have been loved in return.

[3] Many of Po Chü-i's best known poems, for example
the 'Lazy Man's Song' and 'Fishing in the Wei River,'
were written during his Three Years Mourning, which
covered the years A.D. 811–813.

him a period for study and reflection, for writing at last the book that he had planned and never found time to begin, for repairing a life ravaged by official banqueting, a constitution exhausted by the joint claims of concubinage and matrimony.

An allowance was usually granted to support the mourner during this long holiday, and strange though this institution may at first sight appear to be, I am certain that if it were established in the West, civil servants would cling to it as tenaciously as did the bureaucracy of ancient China.

It may be noted, before leaving the subject of mourning, that what chiefly distinguishes Chinese mourning is the inordinate length of the mourning period. So lengthy an observance, carried out by so large a proportion of the population (and from the 1st century B.C. onwards it was, during many periods, actually practised by the whole official class), finds no parallel elsewhere. In many parts of the world, ten days has been considered sufficient; occasionally three months or a hundred days is the period of mourning, particularly in the case of important people. Even in Australia, where some very long mourning periods occur, I have seen none mentioned which extends into the third year. As regards the nature of the observances, however, China is not at all exceptional. Among the many score of practices which are mentioned in ritual literature or referred to in anecdotes, there is hardly one which is not familiar elsewhere. Two widely spread practices are mentioned in the following passage of Mencius: Tsêng Hsi, the father of Master Tsêng, was fond of jujubes, and after his death Master Tsêng could not bring himself to eat jujubes. 'Which taste nicer,' said the disciple Kung-sun Ch'ou, 'mince and roast-meat or jujubes?' 'Mince and roast-meat, to be sure,' said Mencius. 'How was it then,' asked Kung-sun Ch'ou, 'that Master Tsêng was willing to eat mince and roast-meat, but would not eat jujubes?' 'Because,' said Mencius, 'mince and roast-meat are commonly liked, whereas a taste for jujubes is peculiar. In the same way we avoid the personal name of the deceased, but not his surname. The surname is something that he has in common with others; the personal name is peculiar to him.' The avoidance of food particularly liked by the deceased figures here as a preference dictated rather by sentiment than by ritual obligation. Similarly we are told[1] that among the Mafulu of British New Guinea, if a mourner prefers, he may abstain from a favourite food of the deceased instead of wearing the customary mourning necklace. Among the Koita,[2] however, the mourner is ritually obliged to abstain from the favourite food of the deceased for six months.

Avoidance of the name of the deceased, observed by many societies in North America, Oceania, Australia and Africa, has a curious accidental utility in China. It often happens that a study of the name-avoidances followed in a text will reveal its date. Thus the ritualist plays into the hands of the historian.

The country of T'êng maintained a precarious existence, threatened from the north by Ch'i and from the south by Ch'u. Apart from his usual discourse on Government by Goodness, almost identical with that pronounced at other and greater Courts, the further conversations of Mencius with duke Wên of T'êng are concerned with foreign policy.

'T'êng,' said the duke, 'is a small country, sand-

[1] R. W. Williamson, The Mafulu, p. 247 (1912).
[2] C. G. Seligman, The Melanesians, p. 164.

wiched between Ch'i and Ch'u. Which ought I to serve, Ch'i or Ch'u?' 'Upon policies of that kind,' said Mencius, 'I can give no opinion. But if I must needs speak, there is one course that I would urge upon you. Dig out your moats, heighten your walls and guard them along with your people. Show that you are ready to die, and your people will not desert you. So much at least you may do.'

'I hear,' said the duke on another occasion, 'that the men of Ch'i are fortifying Hsieh[1] and am very much alarmed. What course ought I to pursue?' 'Of old,' said Mencius, 'when king T'ai dwelt in Pin, the men of Ti[2] attacked him. He withdrew from Pin and settled at the foot of Mount Ch'i. He would have been glad enough to stay where he was, but he had no choice in the matter. Do right yourself, and in days to come there will certainly be among your descendants one that will become a True King. A gentleman "when he makes the framework, leaves a loose thread hanging";[3] for he thinks of those who are to continue his task. Whether you fail or succeed depends upon Heaven. What other States do is their concern; yours is to do what is right with all your strength. That is all.'

And again; 'T'êng is a small country,' said the duke Wên. 'We have done our utmost to meet the demands of the large countries, but they are not satisfied. What course ought I to pursue?' 'Of old,' said Mencius, 'when king T'ai dwelt in Pin, the men of Ti attacked him. He offered them hides and silks; but they were not satisfied. He offered them dogs and

[1] Hsieh was fortified in 322 B.C.

[2] Regarded as barbarians.

[3] Metaphor of making straw sandals?

horses; but they were not satisfied. He offered them pearls and jade; but they were not satisfied. At last he assembled the elders of Pin and addressed them, saying, "What the men of Ti want is my land. I have heard it said, 'A gentleman cannot suffer that what supplies the people with their food should be allowed to compass their ruin.' My friends, you will do well enough without your king. The time has come for me to leave you."

'So he left Pin, crossed Mount Liang, built a village at the foot of Mount Ch'i and settled there. The people of Pin said, "He is a good man; we should do ill to lose him." And they went in a band, like people flocking to market. Some say, of course, that what has been kept for generation after generation cannot be thus disposed of by one individual, and that he ought to lay down his life rather than go away. It is for you, my lord, to choose between these two.'

Mencius and the King of Sung

A rumour seems to have got about, probably soon after the annexation of Yen, that the small State of Sung, which lay between Wei and Ch'u, was about to put into practice Kingly Government, that is to say, Government by Goodness (*jên*). The news was brought to Mencius by the disciple Wan Chang, who told him that the countries of Ch'i and Ch'u were displeased by what was going on in Sung and were preparing to attack.

The ruler of Sung at this time was king Yen, of whom surprising things are told us by the historian

Ssu-ma Ch'ien.[1] 'In the east he defeated Ch'i, capturing five castles; in the south he defeated Ch'u, taking three hundred leagues of their land; in the west he defeated Wei . . .' That so small a country as Sung should have thus defeated three of the most powerful States in China is hard to believe. What follows is obviously mythological: 'King Yen filled a leather sack with blood, hung it up and shot arrows at it, saying that he was shooting at Heaven; he abandoned himself to wine and women, and when his ministers reproved him he shot at them with his bow.'

Shooting at a sack filled with blood or some other form of target hung aloft as a symbol of Heaven is a widely spread folk-lore theme. In the Mohammedan world the archer is Nimrod; in early China, the Shang king Wu-i.[2] Nimrod was a tyrant who conquered the whole earth; Heaven alone defied him. Many of his subjects, however, including his son Abraham, still worshipped the God of Heaven and were aghast at his iniquities. He therefore decided to make war upon God and become King of Heaven as well as of Earth. He built a great tower (the Tower of Babel) from the top of which he shot an arrow at God. The arrow fell down again, dripping with blood. But Nimrod suddenly became grey and old. Too feeble to move, he lay there till a host of ants devoured him.

The stories of king Yen's atrocities were merely anti-Sung propaganda, put about by the States which intended to partition Sung. A source[3] about a hundred years earlier than the history of Ssu-ma Ch'ien makes this quite clear: 'The king of Ch'in, wanting to attack

[1] Ch. 38. Ssu-ma Ch'ien died c. 80 B.C.
[2] Traditional date, 1198–1195 B.C.
[3] *Chan Kuo Ts'ê*, Yen stories, I.

An-i (in Wei) and fearing that Ch'i would come to the help of Wei, slandered the king of Sung in a message to the king of Ch'i, saying: "The king of Sung is unprincipled. He has made a wooden image of me and shoots at its face.[1] His country does not border on mine and is too far off for me to be able to send an army to attack him. If you would oblige me by destroying Sung on my behalf, I should be quite as happy to see his kingdom in your hands as in mine." Therefore he captured An-i[2] and allowed the blame for the destruction of Sung to fall upon Ch'i.'

Elsewhere[3] in the same book an incitement against Sung is put into the mouth of Su Ch'in:[4] 'I have heard it said that it is the duty of a king who aspires to the praise of the world to punish tyrants, suppress disorders, remove the unprincipled and attack the unrighteous. The king of Sung shoots at Heaven, lashes the earth, has cast bronze figures of all the rulers and makes them wait upon him in the latrine, nudging their arms and twitching their noses. No such iniquity has ever before been witnessed under Heaven. If your Majesty (the king of Ch'i) does not slay him, your reputation will suffer.'

Here, finally, is an account from the same book of how the king of Sung's overweening ambitions originated:

During his reign a sparrow gave birth to a falcon in a corner of the city wall. The Grand Scribe was told to find out what this portended.

[1] A similar enormity is attributed to the tyrant Chou.
[2] A town in Wei.
[3] Yen stories, I, 10 pages earlier.
[4] Legendary protagonist of the Collective Security policy.

'Great born of small,
Means dominion over all,'

he reported. The king of Sung was delighted. He thereupon destroyed the States of T'êng and Hsieh and annexed all the territory north of the river Huai. Growing
more and more confident in himself and intending to
establish himself as master of all China without further
delay, he shot arrows at Heaven, scourged the Earth,
destroyed the Holy Ground and burnt the Millet Sheaf,
saying that all spirits and divinities were subject to his
power. The elders of Sung and the ministers that sought
to admonish him he mocked at; he made a faceless hat
to show to those that were too bold.[1] He split a hunch-
back's hump and cut open the shin of a wayfarer who
was crossing a stream early in the morning.[2] His subjects
were in consternation. The king of Ch'i, hearing of all
this, attacked him, and the people of Sung making no
attempt to defend their walls fled in every direction.
The king of Sung took refuge in the house of his minister
Ni Hou, but was caught and put to death.

Even Dr. Legge,[3] writing over two thousand years
later, calls king Yen 'entirely worthless and oppressive'; such is the long-range power of propaganda.
The aim of these stories (which have no doubt been
much romanticized and exaggerated by the compilers
of the *Chan Kuo Ts'ê*) was of course to represent the
attack on Sung as a Righteous War, an authorized
chastisement, similar to those by which the virtuous

[1] The text seems to be corrupt. In the *Hsin Hsü* it runs
'he made a headless coffin to show . . . ,' which is
equally obscure.
[2] This is one of the atrocities attributed to the tyrant
Chou; he is said to have done it to an old man to see
whether it was true that old men have no marrow in
their bones.
[3] *Mencius*, p. 147.

kings of antiquity destroyed the tyrants Chieh and
Chou.

The duty of the other States to 'punish' any State
which was being badly ruled is strongly emphasized
by the Confucians and was acknowledged (though
less emphatically) by their rivals the Mohists. But
whereas when an individual was accused of crime,
there existed an elaborate machinery by which to discover whether the allegation was well-founded, there
was no inter-State Court which could investigate
charges against a government, and the Righteous
War principle became merely a moral cloak under
which to cover acts of aggression. It was in fact a
mechanism, familiar enough today, for bridging the
gap between the amoralism of those who actually
handle the affairs of a State and the inconvenient
idealism of the masses.

The disciple Wan Chang was dismayed by the fate
of Sung. Here was a small State which was attempting to put into practice Kingly Government, that is
to say government by Goodness, as advocated by
Mencius. According to the teaching of Mencius the
result should have been that all the other States in
China immediately put themselves under the leader-
ship of Sung. In point of fact, quite the opposite
had happened. Two of the largest States, Ch'i and
Ch'u, after violent onslaughts of propaganda against
Sung, were about to lead their armies against it.
How, asked Wan Chang, did Mencius explain this
apparent reversal of his principle?

Mencius replied by reiterating the stories of legendary ancient kings who had won the support of everyone
under Heaven by putting into practice in their own
small territory the humane precepts of Kingly Government. If Sung had failed to win such allegiance,

it could only be because Sung 'was not in point of fact practising Kingly Government or anything of the kind. For if the king of Sung were indeed practising such government, everyone within the Four Seas would raise his head and gaze towards him, wanting to have him and no other as lord and king. Then, mighty though the lands of Ch'i and Ch'u may be, what would Sung have to fear from them?'

To what extent Sung was attempting to practise Government by Goodness, as defined by Mencius, we have no means of judging. The interest of this passage to us is that it illustrates the overwhelming validity of the legendary past, even when confronted with recalcitrant facts of the moment. Mencius was at this time either in Sung or in any case not far off; yet instead of discussing or trying to ascertain what was actually happening in Sung, he cites legends of remote antiquity to prove that what is asserted to be happening now and close at hand cannot really be happening.

It is this ostrich-like attitude to 'the actual facts of the world as it now exists' that brought Confucianism into discredit as a practical morality and paved the way for the Realists.

Mencius and the King of Ch'i

The ambition of king Hsüan of Ch'i (319–301 B.C.),[1] like that of other Chinese rulers of the time, was to

[1] This chronology, different from that found in the current chronological tables, is now generally accepted. See Maspero, La Cronologie des rois de Ts'i, T"oung Pao, 1927.

found a hegemony, to dominate all the other States, to become what was called a *po*, a Senior Baron. Regarding Mencius as a learned man, versed in the history of the past, the king naturally questioned him about former hegemons, and the means by which they attained their position. But the Confucians refused to accept such dictators as models of kingship. According to them, the *po* wins his position merely by physical force; whereas the True King conquers the world by goodness. So when king Hsüan asked about the statecraft of the great hegemons, Mencius quickly changed the subject, and offered instead to tell him about True Kingship.

'What course must I pursue in order to become a True King?' asked Hsüan. 'Constitute yourself the protector of the common people,' said Mencius, 'and nothing can stop you becoming King.' 'I am afraid,' said Hsüan, 'I am not the right sort of person to be a "protector of the common people." '

'You are,' said Mencius.

'How do you know that I am?' asked the king.

'From the following story,' said Mencius, 'which was told me by the courtier Hu Ho. "The king," said he, "was sitting up in the hall, when a man leading a bull passed through the courtyard below. 'Where are you taking the bull?' asked the king. 'To be slaughtered,' said the man. 'We are using its blood to consecrate a new bell.' 'Let it go!' said the king. 'I can't bear to see a poor frightened, harmless thing like that going to its death.' 'Your Majesty means that the bell is not to be consecrated?' asked the man. 'Of course it will have to be consecrated,' said the king. 'You can use a sheep instead.' " That was the story I heard. But perhaps you will say it is not true.'

'It is perfectly true,' said the king. 'Very well then,' said Mencius, 'such feelings as you showed on that

occasion are all that a ruler needs in order to become a
True King. As a matter of fact, most people thought
that you behaved like this out of meanness. But I knew
quite well that it was because you could not bear the
idea of this creature being slaughtered.' 'Indeed it was,'
said the king. 'Did people really say . . . ? Of course,
Ch'i is not a large country; but it would be strange
indeed if I were to grudge the loss of one bull. No, it
was just as you said. I could not bear to see a poor,
frightened harmless thing going to its death. That was
why I suggested using a sheep instead.' 'You can hardly
be surprised that people thought you grudged the bull,'
said Mencius; 'for you were quite willing to sacrifice a
smaller animal instead, and this made your true feelings
very difficult for them to understand. "If the king were
really pained at the idea of an innocent creature being
led to the slaughter, this would apply just as well to a
sheep as to a bull," that is what they must have said.'

The king smiled. 'I wonder what it was exactly that I
did feel,' he said. 'I really did not grudge the expense.
But I see now that my having proposed a sheep instead
made it quite natural that people should think I grudged
it.'

'Never mind,' said Mencius. 'That is the way that pity
works. You had seen the bull and had not seen the
sheep. That is how a gentleman should feel about
animals. If he has seen them alive, he cannot bear to see
them die. If he has heard their cries, he cannot bear to
eat their flesh. That is why a gentleman never goes too
near the kitchen.' This pleased the king. 'It says in the
Songs,'[1] he replied,

'The feelings that others have
By inference I measure.

This applies very well to you. It was I who did this
thing; but when I came to look into myself and search

[1] Mao. 198, 4.

for the reason, I could not understand my own feelings. But as soon as you explained them to me, something in my own heart at once clicked. Tell me, how can feelings of this sort help me to become a True King?'

'Suppose,' said Mencius, 'someone were to state to you that he was strong enough to lift three thousand catties, but not strong enough to lift one feather; or that his sight was so good that he could see the tip of a hair, but that he could not see a cartload of faggots, would you believe him?' 'No,' said the king. 'How can it be then,' asked Mencius, 'that your softness of heart is so great that it extends even to animals, and yet fails to bring any practical benefit to the people over whom you rule? In the case of the man who "cannot lift one feather," we can only say that he could if he would use his strength; in the case of the man who "cannot see a cartload of faggots," we can only say that he could if he used his eyes. If then your people do not find in you a protector, this can only be because you do not use your softness of heart. Thus if you have not risen to greatness as a True King, it is because you choose not to do so, not because you are unable to do so.'

'What is the difference in actual practice between choosing not to and not being able?' asked the king. 'Well, for example,' said Mencius, 'if someone said to you, "Take the Great Mountain under your arm and leap with it across the Northern Sea," and you say, "I am unable to," that really is being unable. But if someone older than you asks you to crack his joints and you say "I am unable to," that can in fact only be because you do not choose to. There can be no question of not being able to.

'Thus your failure to become a True King is not like the case of jumping over the Northern Sea with the Great Mountain under one's arm. It is like refusing to crack an old man's joints. . . . You have but to push your softness of heart far enough and you will become protector of all within the Four Seas. Restrict it, and your own wife and children will be more than you can protect. It was so with the Ancients. If they far surpassed ordinary man, this was for one reason only: that which was good in them they continually pushed on to wider applications. But though your softness of heart makes you deal tenderly with animals, you do not go on to apply it in any way to your dealings with those over whom you rule. How is this? For example, you collect vast equipments of war, endanger your officers and ministers, arouse resentment among the rulers of other States. Are you any the happier for this?' 'No,' said the king. 'But I do not do it for pleasure. There are certain things that I want very much, and they cannot be got in any other way.' 'I should like to hear what those things are,' said Mencius.

The king smiled to himself, but did not answer.

'Perhaps,' said Mencius, 'you want richer and sweeter food to eat or lighter and warmer clothes to wear or brighter stuffs to look at or better music to listen to. Or perhaps you have not enough flatterers and favourites about you to carry out your orders. But those are things that the officers of your Court could easily supply. It cannot be to get these things that you prepare for war.' 'No, it is not for such things as that,' said the king. 'Well then,' said Mencius, 'it is not hard to guess what it is that you so much desire. You want to extend your territories, make vassals of Ch'in and Ch'u, rule the Middle Kingdom and hold down the barbarians on every side. I can only tell you that to seek ends such as these by the means that you employ is like trying to get fish off a tree.'

'Is it as bad as that?' said the king. 'As a matter of fact, it is worse,' said Mencius. 'For if you try to get fish from a tree, though you will certainly get no fish, there will at any rate be no evil consequences. But the quest of such ends as you have named by the means that you employ, if carried out with determination, cannot but lead to calamity.' 'In what way?' asked the king. 'Suppose,' said Mencius, 'that the men of Tsou[1] went to war with the men of Ch'u,[2] who do you think would win?' 'The men of Ch'u would win,' said the king. 'Very well then,' said Mencius, 'let us accept that the small cannot contend with the large, the few with the many, the weak with the strong. Now the land that is within the Four Seas has nine divisions, each a thousand leagues square. The territories of Ch'i may, taken together, amount to as much as one of these nine divisions. Is it not clear that one part has about as much chance of subduing the other eight as Tsou has of beating Ch'u?

'No; there is nothing for it but to go back to the root of the matter. If you were this day to set up a form of government founded upon Goodness, at once all the officers under Heaven would want to be enrolled in your Court, all the ploughmen would want to plough up your freelands, all the merchants and tradesmen would want to bring their goods to your market, all travellers would want to use your roads, and all those anywhere under Heaven who had grievances against their ruler would want to lay their complaints before you. All would be so bent upon coming to you that no power could stop them.'

'I am not a clever man,' said the king, 'and all this is rather beyond me. But I hope that, if you keep me up to the mark and tell me clearly just what I am to do, I may be able despite my dullness to put your instructions into practice.'

'It is only people of the upper classes,' said Mencius, 'who can maintain fixed principles of right and wrong even if deprived of a settled livelihood. The common people, if deprived of a settled livelihood, lose all fixed principles, and when this happens they become completely licentious and depraved—there is nothing that they will not do. To allow them to fall into the net of

[1] A very small State.
[2] A very large State.

crime, and then proceed to inflict penalties upon them, this is trapping them as one traps wild animals. Is it thinkable that one who sets out to rule by Goodness could ever do such a thing as to set a trap for his people?

'No; an enlightened ruler in regulating the livelihood of his people will make sure that in the first place they are well enough off to look after their parents and able to support wife and child, that in good years they get as much as they can eat at every meal and that in bad years they shall at least be in no danger of starvation. Only when this has been assured does he "gallop on to goodness," and the people will have no difficulty in following him.

'As things are now, the livelihood of the people is not so regulated that any of these things is assured. With means so scanty as to keep them in constant dread of starvation, how can they be expected to have cultivated manners and morals?

'If you really want to carry this thing through, I must again recommend you to go to the root of the matter: for each family, five acres[1] of orchard, planted with mulberry-trees; and no one over fifty will lack silk clothing. Let them have chickens, pigs, dogs, and swine to breed, and if they are given sufficient time to look after them no one over seventy will go without flesh to eat. Give each family a hundred acres for its crops, and if they are allowed enough time to work the land, a household of eight persons will never suffer from hunger. Be sure that at the schools and colleges stress is laid upon the duty of children to parents and of the young to their elders in the same generation, and grey-haired men will no longer be seen going about the roads with burdens on their backs. One whose subjects wear silk and eat flesh when they are old, within whose frontiers the common people are never famished, never cold, cannot fail to become a True King.'

[1] An acre was 300 paces square.

Mencius went to P'ing-lu and said to the governor of the town: 'Supposing one of your bodyguard failed three times in one day to appear at his post, would you dismiss him or not?' 'I should not wait till the third time,' said the governor. 'Yet you yourself,' said Mencius, 'have failed to appear at your post time after time. Whenever the crops fail and there is famine in the land, the old and feeble among your people drop by the wayside and are rolled into the nearest ditch; while the able-bodied escape, some this way, some that, drifting off in their thousands.' 'It is not possible for me to do anything about it,' said the governor. 'Supposing,' said Mencius, 'someone undertakes to look after another man's cattle and sheep, he will make certain first of all that he can secure pasturing ground and fodder, and if this turns out to be impossible, I cannot help thinking he will return the cattle and sheep to their owner, rather than stand by and see them perish.'

'In that respect,' said the governor, 'I confess I am at fault.'

Not long afterwards Mencius had an audience with the king of Ch'i. 'I am personally acquainted with five of your city-governors,' he said to the king, 'and the only one who has ever admitted to me that he was in the wrong is K'ung Chü-hsin, governor of P'ing-lu.' He then told the king about his conversation with the governor. 'In this matter,' admitted the king, 'it is I myself who am to blame.'

The Yen Episode

As we have seen above[1] in 314 B.C. Ch'i (the State where Mencius was living) annexed the northern

[1] Page 62.

State of Yen. The ruler of Yen, Tzu K'uai, had handed over the government of the State to his minister Tzu Chih. The new ruler was very unpopular; disorders broke out in Yen, and as the transference of power from a ruler to his minister, though it had occurred in other States, was a technical irregularity, there was a good excuse for invasion of Yen as a 'mission of chastisement,' as a 'righteous war,' undertaken in order to support the Imperial dignity. For in theory it was the Emperor alone who had the right to invest a local ruler.

Mencius's part in the affair was somewhat equivocal. When asked, 'Ought Yen to be chastised?' he replied, 'Yes; Tzu K'uai had no right to give Yen to another, and Tzu Chih had no right to accept Yen from Tzu K'uai.' When the invasion had taken place someone asked Mencius whether he had really advised Ch'i to chastise Yen. He admitted that he said, 'Yen ought to be chastised,' but insisted that if he had been asked who ought to chastise it, he would have said 'One worthy to act as a ministrant of Heaven.'

This however would have been tantamount to saying that Yen ought not to be chastised. For there was no State at the time which Mencius could have regarded as 'worthy to act as a ministrant of Heaven.' Mencius must have known very well that his actual answer could only be interpreted as a recommendation that Ch'i should 'chastise' Yen. It is clear, however, that he was afterwards aghast at the result of the policy he had recommended.

The men of Ch'i attacked Yen and conquered it. King Hsüan of Ch'i consulted Mencius. 'Some of my counsellors,' he said, 'advise me not to annex Yen; but there are others who say I ought to do so, on the ground that if a kingdom of ten thousand war chariots attacks another kingdom of ten thousand war chariots and over-runs it completely in fifty days, such a feat is beyond mere human endeavour; it could only have been achieved with the aid of Heaven. Consequently not to annex Yen would be to flout the will of Heaven and would certainly bring upon us some Heaven-sent disaster. What is your view?' 'If the people of Yen desire Yen to be annexed, then annex it,' said Mencius. . . . 'When, as in this case, a kingdom of ten thousand war chariots attacks a king-dom of ten thousand war chariots and the inhabitants meet the invading army with flagons of drink and baskets of food, there can only be one reason: they see in the invasion a chance of escape from "flood and fire."[1] If then under your rule they find the waters even deeper, the fire more fierce, the whole process will repeat itself;[2] that is all.'

Ch'i annexed Yen, and it was reported that the rulers of the other States were preparing to rescue Yen. 'I hear that many of the other kingdoms are preparing to attack me,' said king Hsüan of Ch'i. 'How am I to deal with them?' . . . 'The ruler of Yen,' said Mencius, 'was mishandling his people. You sent an army to chastise him, and the people of Yen, thinking that you were going to rescue them from "flood and fire," met your armies with flagons of drink and baskets of food. Yet here we are, killing their fathers and elder brothers, making bondsmen of their sons and younger brothers, destroying their ancestral temples, carrying off their precious vessels! What possible justification can there be for all this?

'The formidable strength of Ch'i was always viewed with anxiety by the rest of the world. Now you have doubled its territories, without practising Government by Goodness. That is the surest way to have the whole

[1] Tyrannous rule.

[2] Yen revolted in 312 B.C.; or according to some ac-counts immediately after the conquest in 314.

world up in arms against you. You must send out orders at once that the very old and very young are to be restored to their families and that precious vessels are not to be removed. You must then, after consulting with representative people in Yen, set up a new ruler, and withdraw your troops. If you do this there may still be time to stop this attack.'

The Handling of Sages

The key to Mencius's first reaction to the events in Yen is his profound conservatism. No more than Confucius could he reconcile himself to the fact that the Chou empire and its institutions had long ago been swept away. He was still deeply shocked by infringements upon a constitution that had had no real existence for over four hundred years, and his first thought was one of 'chastisement,' irrespective of the chastiser. This conservatism, by no means common to all the schools of thought in his day, is reflected in his whole view of society as divided into two classes, 'those who are fed,' and 'those who produce food.' The gentlemen, 'those who are fed,' apart from their function as rulers, for which they are of course separately paid, have two claims on the community: they set a pattern of domestic morality and act as custodians of the Way of the Former Kings, 'that those who come afterwards may be able to learn it.'

It cannot be said that in their capacity as custodians of ancient tradition the gentlemen of Mencius's day were very successful. They not only allowed their ancient texts to become so corrupt as to be unintelligible, but also allowed them to be continually supplemented with modern additions. Nor did the cultured classes fulfil this particular function much more successfully in later times. It took them one thousand five hundred years to discover definitely (though there had been dim surmises before) that half the venerated Book of History was a fraud of comparatively late times.

Gentlemen, as we shall see below, work with their minds; peasants with their hands. One cannot help feeling that had not these hand-workers tilled the fields a good deal more efficiently than the mind-workers guarded 'the Way of the Former Kings,' it would have gone hard indeed with China.

It was part of Confucianism, as indeed of traditional thought in general, to believe that a True King could only carry out his task with the help of a Sage Minister. This inspired assistant was a *hsien* ('better'), someone above the normal level of human capacity. Mencius believed himself to be the only man of his generation qualified to play such a part: 'if Heaven wanted to bring peace and order into the world, who is there but myself?' meaning, 'who else is there that Heaven could use as an instrument?' His claim to be supported at public expense was therefore threefold: as an old man, as a 'mind-worker' (an intellectual) and as a *hsien* capable of guiding a monarch into the path of True Kingship.

But a *hsien* is distrustful of Courts and Princes, and unless he is very carefully handled his help cannot be secured. To begin with, he must be summoned in the right way. In this connection Mencius tells more than once the story of duke Ching of Ch'i and his forester. The duke summoned this forester by waving a flag. The forester did not budge. The duke was on the point of having him executed for insubordination, when the forester explained that he ought to have been summoned by the waving of a leather cap, not by the waving of a flag.

If properly approached by a prince who seems likely to put the Way of Former Kings into practice, the *hsien* may consent to come; but the prince's difficulties are still not at an end. He must not expect the wise man to visit him; but on the contrary, behaving as a subject not as a prince, he must humbly present himself at the wise man's lodging. If he failed to do so and allowed the visitor to present himself at Court, there could be no question of the Sage helping him on to the Way of True Kingship; the visit became an ordinary matter of diplomatic courtesy.

The king of Ch'i and Mencius on one occasion became entangled in a strange network of alibis, subterfuges, and fictitious indispositions. Mencius had decided that the king did not mean to visit him and was on the point of showing his displeasure by visiting the king, when a message came from Court: 'I was going to call upon you,' the king said, 'when I unfortunately caught cold. I dare not expose myself to the wind. But tomorrow morning I shall be holding my levée, and perhaps you will give me a chance of seeing you then?' 'Very unfortunately,' replied Mencius, 'I too am unwell and shall not be able to go to Court.'

Next day, however, he went out to pay a visit of condolence. 'Surely,' protested one of his disciples, 'it was a mistake to pay a visit of condolence today, after saying yesterday that you were too unwell to go to Court?' 'Not at all,' said Mencius. 'Yesterday I was ill; today I am better. Why should I not pay a visit of condolence?'[1]

The king sent someone to enquire after Mencius's health, and a doctor arrived. It fell to the disciple Mêng Chung to deal with them. 'Yesterday,' he explained, 'when His Majesty's command arrived, the Master was indisposed and unable to go to Court. This morning he was rather better and at once hurried off to Court. I dare say he is already there.' He then sent several men to waylay Mencius and persuade him to call in at the Court on his way home. They were not successful, and Mencius instead spent the night in hiding at the house of a friend.

Then there was the question of gifts and allowances. Presents of money easily assume the aspect of a bribe. Presents of food may suggest that the Sage is merely being 'fed like a dog or horse.' Lucky indeed was the monarch who could persuade a Sage to accept his support; and once he had done so, he must no longer regard himself as master of his own time. 'What wonder,' said Mencius, 'that the king is not wise! Take now the case of some common plant that is the easiest thing on earth to grow. If you leave it ten days in the cold for every one day that you put it in the sun, there is no plant so hardy that it will live. My interviews with the king are few and far between. When I am not there, my place is taken by those that blow cold upon my work, and even if I have started a few sprouts growing, what becomes of them?'

[1] Mencius overlooks the fact the king might equally say, 'today you are better; why should you not come to Court?'

Great Men

The heroes of the day were men like the Wei general
Kung-sun Yen and the itinerant politician Chang I,
of whom I have spoken above.[1] 'Surely,' said Ching
Ch'un (himself supposed to be an adept in inter-
State intrigue), 'you would consider Kung-sun Yen
and Chang I really great men? They have but to say
one angry word, and all the princes tremble; they
have but to keep quiet for a while, and the whole
world breathes a sigh of relief.' 'What reason is there,'
said Mencius, 'to call them great men? . . . He who
is at home in the great house of the world, stands
firm in the highest place of the world,[2] walks in the
great highways of the world,[3] if successful, lets the
people have the benefit of his success, if unsuccessful,
practises the Way all alone; he whom riches and
honours cannot corrupt nor poverty and obscurity
divert, whom neither threats nor violence itself can
bend—he it is that I call a great man.'

As opposed to the Great Man, the moral hero, is the
'great personage,' surrounded by a pomp and luxury
which should not dazzle the true Confucian: 'Those
who give counsel to a great personage should hold
aloof and pay no heed to the splendours and luxuries
that surround him. Halls hundreds of feet high,
beams projecting a yard from the eaves, these are
things that even if the choice were given us, we

[1] Page 65 and page 63.

[2] Is a man and not a woman or animal.

[3] And not on 'byways.' Cf. *Analects*, VI. 12.

would not choose to have. Vast expanses of food set out, hundreds of men-servants and maid-servants, these are things that, even were the choice given us, we should not choose to have. Wanton revels and carousals, galloping headlong to the hunt with a thousand chariots following, these are things that even if the choice were given us we should not choose. What he has are things that we should not choose; what we have is what the ancients decreed. Why should such men as we stand in awe of such a man as he?'

THE RIVAL SCHOOLS

Mencius's principal opponents were the followers of Mo Tzu and Yang Chu.[1] His references to them are couched in language of irrational and intemperate abuse. He speaks of Mo Tzu, who taught that all men should love one another no less than they loved themselves, as 'abolishing fatherhood,' merely because fathers lose in Mo Tzu's system the unique position they hold in Confucianism. And because Yang Chu held that each individual should perfect himself spiritually and physically, rather than sacrifice himself to the supposed good of the community, Mencius says that the followers of Yang Chu 'abolish prince-hood,' that is to say, do away with all governmental

[1] Mo Tzu flourished c. 420 B.C. Of Yang Chu we know hardly anything.

authority, and that Yang Chu and Mo Tzu both wish
to reduce mankind to the level of wild beasts. It may
be true that animals spend their time perfecting
themselves spiritually; it is certainly not true that
they practise universal love, as recommended by Mo
Tzu. Then quite inconsequently, but apparently still
obsessed by the thought of wild beasts, Mencius
declares that by 'obstructing goodness and duty, the
followers of Mo Tzu and Yang Chu are leading on
wild beasts to devour men.'

Mo Tzu

A good many people outside China have heard of
Confucianism and Taoism; very few know even the
name of Mo Tzu. This is not surprising. The *Analects*
of Confucius are forcible and pointed; at times they
even rise to a sort of austere beauty. Mencius contains some of the subtlest and most vivid passages in
Chinese literature. The Tao Tê Ching (*Lao Tzu*),
most frequently translated of all Chinese books, is
an occultist kaleidoscope, a magic void that the reader
can fill with what images he will; *Chuang Tzu* is one
of the most entertaining as well as one of the pro-
foundest books in the world. Whereas *Mo Tzu* is
feeble, repetitive (and I am not referring to the fact
that many of the chapters occur in alternative forms),
heavy, unimaginative and unentertaining, devoid of a
single passage that could possibly be said to have wit,
beauty or force. Of course, part of the obscurity of
Mo Tzu in the West is due to the fact that he was
till recently very little studied even in China. But he
has been accessible in European languages for a

considerable time.[1] If Mo Tzu is neglected in Europe it is because he expounds his on the whole rather sympathetic doctrines with a singular lack of aesthetic power.

Moreover these doctrines strike us as curiously heterogeneous. Both Confucianism and Taoism express attitudes to life with which we are familiar. We could even roughly divide our own friends and acquaintances into Confucians and Taoists. But who has ever known a Mohist or can adequately imagine what it felt like to be one? 'Universal love' sounds well enough, though one is somewhat disconcerted to find that people are to be 'awed into it by punishments and fines.'[2] 'No aggression' too sounds excellent, till one reads that 'punitive expeditions' do not count as wars. Hanging rather loosely from the bunch we find the doctrine of Free Will. If people believe in Fate, they say 'The rich are fated to be rich, the poor are fated to be poor. What is the use of bestirring oneself?' And then what will happen? 'The countryman will be lazy at his ploughing and reaping, his planting and tilling, the wife at her twisting and spinning, her stitching and weaving, the king and his ministers at the hearing of lawsuits and handling of public affairs. The world will soon be in a great muddle.' The Confucians, on the contrary, had the subtlety to see that belief in Fate is perfectly compatible with energetic action. When things go well, the gentleman does not 'talk about Fate,' but when they go badly he 'recognizes Fate,' content in the knowledge that he has done his best.

[1] Alfred Forke's translation of the whole book appeared in 1922; an English translation by Y. P. Mei, omitting only the chapters on logic and some later additions, was published several years later.

[2] XVI, near the end.

We shall see[1] that Mo Tzu made a broad distinction between what is 'beneficial' and what is 'harmful.' Under the heading harmful he included all lavish ritual expenditure, in particular the wholesale waste of property that accompanied an orthodox Chinese burial. 'Even when an ordinary and undistinguished person dies,' says Mo Tzu, 'the expenses of the funeral are such as to reduce the family almost to beggary; and when a ruler dies, by the time enough gold and jade, pearls and precious stones have been found to lay by the body, wrappings of fine stuffs to bind round it, chariots and horses to bury with it in the tomb, and the necessary quantity of tripods and drums under their coverings and awnings, of jars and bowls on tables and stands, of halberds, swords, feather-work screens and banners, objects in ivory and in leather, have been made . . . the treasuries of the State are completely exhausted. Morover in the case of an Emperor, sometimes several hundred and never less than twenty or thirty of his servants are slain to follow him; for a general or principal minister sometimes twenty or thirty persons are slain, and never less than four or five.'

On top of this waste of life and wealth comes that 'long interruption of business,' as Mo Tzu calls it— the Three Years Mourning. 'The mourner,' says Mo Tzu, 'howls and sobs continuously on one note, soaks with falling tears his coat of rough cloth and his token of hemp,[2] lives in a hovel,[3] sleeps on a straw-

---

[1] See p. 135.

[2] What is referred to here is the hempen badge worn in lieu of a belt.

[3] Built as a lean-to against the side of the grave-mound. This practice is found in parts of Melanesia and Australia.

mattress with a clod of earth for his pillow. He continually and obstinately refuses food, till he is on the point of starvation, wears so little clothing that he is cold, his face becomes sunken and wrinkled, his skin sallow, his sight grows dim, his hearing dull, his limbs become so feeble that he cannot use them. A high officer must carry this so far that he cannot stand without being supported and cannot walk without a stick. Such is the observance of the Three Years Mourning. If these prescriptions were adopted and this rule carried out by ministers and officials they could not control their departments and offices, or see to it that new ground was brought under cultivation and stores and granaries were well stocked. If farmers observed these rules, they could not, rising early and coming back late at night, devote themselves as they should to ploughing, reaping, planting and tilling. If craftsmen observed these rules, they would be prevented from making boats and carriages, furniture and dishes. If wives observed these rules they could not, rising early and going to bed late, devote themselves as they should to spinning, hemp-twisting, or the weaving of silk and cloth. . . .

'Indeed, if elaborate burial and long mourning are encouraged by a government, the country will be impoverished, its population decline, and its administration be thrown into confusion. If the country is impoverished, its offerings of grain and liquor will be of low quality; if the population declines, there will be an insufficient number of people properly to serve God (Shang Ti) and the spirits; if the administration is in confusion, offerings and sacrifices will not be made at the proper times and seasons. If then the government encourages a practice that hinders the service of God and the Spirits, then God and the

Spirits will point at these people from on high, saying: "Is the existence of such men really of any
advantage to us, or is it of no advantage at all; indeed,
is it preferable to let them go on existing, or not to
let them go on existing?" Then God and the Spirits
will send down upon them crimes,[1] pestilences, calamities and afflictions, and will forsake them for ever.'

This sounds very Biblical. It is indeed the language
of early Chou times and shows Mo Tzu's archaistic
bent. The conception of God on High is exactly that
of the early Songs and of the inscriptions on early
Chou bronzes.

In a passage unusually spritely for him[2] Mo Tzu
pours ridicule on the Summons to the Soul, an
essential element in early Chinese death rites: 'When
a parent dies, after the corpse has been laid out, but
before it has been put in the coffin, they go up on to
the roof, peer down into the well, scoop out the rats'
holes, examine the washing-tub, to look for the deceased. If they really expect to find him, they must be
consummate fools; while if they look knowing quite
well that he is not there, what humbugs they must
be!'

Mo Tzu condemned 'music.' But the Chinese word
in question had a much wider sense than our term
'music.' What Mo Tzu had in mind were elaborate
and costly dance rituals, demanding expensive cos-
tumes, the maintenance of large companies of dancers
and musicians, all of which were paid out of the
public funds. The orchestras included sets of metal

[1] Literally 'nets.' Sin is conceived of by many early peo-
ples as a net in which God snares men. See The Book of
Songs, p. 331.

[2] The passage of course may be the work of his followers.

bells on vast stands for the construction of which
special levies were exacted:

'Duke K'ang[1] of Ch'i used to get up performances
of the Wan[2] dance. The Wan dancers are not allowed
to wear ordinary clothes or to eat common food. It
is said that if they did not eat fine food and drink
fine liquors, their complexions would not be worth
looking at, and if they did not wear fine clothes, their
movements would not be worth watching. So they
are fed on nothing but meat and the choicest rice,
clothed in nothing but patterned and embroidered
stuffs. These people take no part in the production
either of clothing or of food, but are clothed and fed
by the industry of others. It is clear then that if rulers
and their ministers encourage musical performances,
the common people will go short of food and clothing, so great is the drain of such performances upon
their resources. That is why Mo Tzu said that it is
wrong to go in for music.'

Such performances and indeed all the amusements
and pleasures of the Court were countenanced by the
Confucians only on the condition that the people
were allowed to share in them. In the following passage Mencius is speaking of music; but he also
discusses hunting, and his moral is that the people
will only tolerate the contrast between their own
sordid existence and the brilliant life of the Court,
if the ruler is seen to realize that they are capable
of enjoying the same pleasures as himself, and is willing to let them share in these pleasures:

'I have just had an audience with the king,' said
Chuang Pao, a minister at the Ch'i Court, to Mencius

[1] Reigned from 404–391 B.C.
[2] See The Book of Songs, p. 338.

one day, 'and he talked to me about his great fondness for music.[1] He asked me whether I thought it a good thing that a king should be fond of music, and I did not know what to reply.'[2] 'If the king were very fond of music,' said Mencius, 'there would soon be little amiss with the country of Ch'i.' Not long afterwards Mencius had an audience. 'Your Majesty,' he said, 'was telling Chuang Pao the other day how fond you are of music, or so I understood.' 'I did not mean,' said the king, blushing, 'that I can manage to like the music of the Former Kings, my ancestors. What I like is the popular music of the day.' 'If your Majesty were fond enough of music,' said Mencius, 'there would soon be little amiss with the country of Ch'i, no matter whether it was modern music or ancient music.' 'Please explain yourself,' said the king. 'Which is the pleasanter,' asked Mencius, 'to enjoy music alone or in company?' 'In company,' said the king. 'With just a few others, or with a great many?' asked Mencius. 'With a great many,' said the king. 'Well then,' said Mencius. 'I think I can explain to your Majesty my views about music. Suppose when you gave a musical performance, your subjects hearing the noise of your bells and drums, the sound of your pipes and flutes, were with one accord to feel headache, frown and say to one another, "All our king cares about is making music; else he would not bring us to such extremities that father and son cannot meet, elder brother and younger brother, wife and child are torn apart and scattered over the land. . . ."[3] What would be the reason that they felt like this? It could

---

[1] It should be remembered that the word includes dancing and miming, and that the word for 'pleasure' is written with the same character.

[2] These two clauses are accidentally inverted in the original.

[3] Owing to military levies, forced labour and so on.

happen only because you did not share your pleasure with the people.

'Suppose again, when you gave a musical performance, your subjects hearing the noise of your bells and drums, the sound of your pipes and flutes, were with one accord to feel delighted and say to one another with beaming countenances, "Our King must be in fairly good health, otherwise he would not be giving this performance. . . ." What would be the reason of their feeling so very differently in this case? It could happen only because you shared your pleasures with the people. Were your Majesty but to share your pleasures with those over whom you rule, you would become a king indeed.'[1]

The idea that the dead are pleased and placated by the performance of music and dances, so evident in earlier literature,[2] or that they may feel slighted if not accorded an elaborate burial is not found in Mo Tzu. But he makes them part of a threefold sanction for moral conduct. There are, he says, three classes of spirit (kuei): heavenly spirits, the spirits and divinities (shên) of hills and waters, and spirits which are the ghosts of dead human beings.[3] The existence of heavenly spirits (t'ien kuei), that is to say, of Heaven (t'ien), is not necessary to prove; for t'ien means not only Heaven and 'the sky,' but also 'the weather'; and no one would venture to deny the existence of the weather. With regard to other kinds of spirits the case was quite different. Many of Mo Tzu's contemporaries did not believe in them, and a special section of Mo Tzu is devoted to proving that they indubitably do exist. To this end Mo Tzu repeats a number

[1] A True King, ruler of all China. The kings of Ch'i had merely usurped the title of king.
[2] See The Book of Songs, p. 225, line 4.
[3] XXXI, near the end.

of ghost-stories from old chronicles and histories; for example:

King Hsüan of Chou killed his minister, the lord of Tu,[1] who had done no wrong. 'If the dead are indeed not conscious,' said the lord of Tu, 'this is the end of the matter. But if the dead are conscious, before three years are out the king shall know it to his cost.' During the third year king Hsüan assembled all his barons and went hunting in his great park, accompanied by many hundred chariots and many thousand men on foot, filling all the countryside. Exactly at noon the lord of Tu appeared in an unpainted chariot drawn by white horses. His coat and hat were red, there was a red bow in his hand and a red arrow upon the bow-string. He pursued the king and shot at him as he stood in his chariot. The arrow entered at the king's heart and shattered his spine. He sank down in his chariot, and died face downwards upon his bow-case. This was not merely witnessed by all the men of Chou who were present at the hunt, but heard of by all such as were far away; and it was duly narrated in the chronicles of Chou, that princes might teach their ministers and fathers might warn their sons, saying: 'Be warned, take care! He who slays an innocent man is doomed to disaster, so sharp and fierce is the vengeance of the spirits!' Judging from what is written in those chronicles, there cannot be any doubt at all that spirits exist.

The dead punish those who have wronged them when they were alive. Upon whom then does Heaven, which cannot have personal grievances, vent its wrath? According to Mo Tzu, upon those who do not practise universal Love. By this he does not, as we have seen, mean a vague general philanthropy. He

[1] South of the modern Sian Fu. The execution took place according to traditional chronology in 783 B.C.

uses the term in a controversial sense, opposing it to the principle of the Confucians, according to which people were to be loved on a decreasing scale, beginning with parents, who were to be loved a great deal, and ending with remote persons such as the men of Yüeh, who were to be loved much less. Such a principle, said Mo Tzu, was the cause of all the wars and dissensions that were then rending China. If men loved the citizens of other States as much as they loved their parents, they would not consent to 'slay or enslave the grown men, carry off wives and children, horses and cattle, destroy their cities, upset their shrines.' The whole trouble indeed comes from having one moral standard in dealing with 'what is near' and another in dealing with 'what is far.'

If a ruler attacks a neighbouring country, slays its inhabitants, carries off its cattle and horses, its millet and rice and all its chattels and possessions, his deed is recorded on strips of bamboo or rolls of silk, carved upon metal and stone, inscribed upon bells and tripods, that in after days are handed down to his sons and grandsons. 'No one,' he boasts, 'ever took such spoils as I have done.' But suppose some private person attacked the house next door, slew the inhabitants, stole their dogs and pigs, their grain and their clothing, and then made a record of his deed on strips of bamboo or rolls of silk and wrote inscriptions about it on his dishes and bowls, that they might be handed down in his family for generations to come, boasting that no one ever stole so much as he, would that be all right? 'No,' said the lord of Lu. 'And looking at the matter as you have put it, I see that many things which the world regards as all right are not necessarily right at all.'

But, like the Confucians, Mo Tzu believed in the Righteous War, in which a good king, at the command of Heaven, punishes a bad one, and he even condemns the chivalrous etiquette of warfare,[1] upheld by the Confucians, on the ground that it handicaps the virtuous in their stern task: 'Suppose there is a country which is being persecuted and oppressed by its rulers, and a Sage ruler in order to rid the world of this pest raises an army and sets out to punish the evil-doers. If, when he has won a victory, he conforms to the doctrine of the Confucians, he will issue an order to his troops saying: "Fugitives are not to be pursued, an enemy who has lost his helmet is not to be shot at; if a chariot overturns, you are to help the occupants to right it"[2]—if this is done, the violent and disorderly will escape with their lives and the world will not be rid of its pest. These people have carried out wholesale massacres of men and women, and done great harm in their day. There could be no greater injustice than that they should be allowed to escape.'

Contrast with this the following anecdote from Mencius.

The men of Chêng sent Tzu-cho Ju-tzu to attack Wei. Wei sent Yu-kung Ssu to drive him away. Tzu-cho Ju-tzu said, 'today my fever is upon me and I cannot hold my bow. I am a dead man.' And he asked his groom, 'Whom have they sent to repel me?' 'Yu-kung Ssu,' said his groom. 'Then,' said Tzu-cho Ju-tzu, 'I am a live man.' 'But this Yu-kung Ssu is the best archer in Wei,' said the groom. 'How can you say that you are a "live man"?' 'For this reason,' said Tzu-cho Ju-tzu: 'Yu-kung Ssu learnt archery from Yin-kung T'o, and Yin-kung T'o

---

[1] For an admirable description of this etiquette, see Granet, *La Civilisation Chinoise*, p. 316 seq.

[2] This last sentence is corrupt, and the sense can only be guessed at.

learnt it from me. Now Yin-kung T'o was a decent man and I am sure that he would not have made friends with anyone who was not also a decent man.'

'Why is your bow not in your hands?' asked Yu-kung Ssu when he arrived. 'Today my fever is upon me,' said Tzu-cho Ju-tzu, 'and I cannot hold my bow.' 'My master in archery was Ying-kung T'o,' said Yu-kung Ssu, 'and he learnt it from you. I cannot bring myself to turn an art that I have received from you to your own undoing. Nevertheless what I am here to do today is not my business but my prince's, and I cannot neglect it.' So saying he drew his arrows from the quiver and striking them against the wheel of his chariot he knocked off the metal tips, shot four arrows, and then withdrew.

The tenets of Mo Tzu seem to us somewhat ill-assorted, and it is hard to relate them to any familiar outlook or type of temperament. But when we turn from theory to practice, from controversial essays to stories of Mohism in action, we are conscious at once of a definite and recognizable atmosphere. The Mohists were an organized body, under the strict control of a leader known as the Grand Master, who enforced absolute obedience to an exacting code of honour and self-sacrifice.[1] Politically they were by no means negligible; for they were specially trained in defensive warfare, and a State which contained a strong Mohist element was not lightly to be attacked. The atmosphere of Mohism in action, its rigid discipline and quixotic ideals, are well illustrated by the following story (*Lü Shih Ch'un Ch'iu*, 111):

[1] 'Wearing coarse hair-cloth and rough clogs, they rested neither by day nor night from the hardship that it was their aim to impose upon themselves, holding that those who were incapable of enduring such a life were not worthy to be called followers of Mo.'—*Chuang Tzu*, 33.

Mêng Shêng, the Grand Master of the Mohists, was on intimate terms with the lord of Yang-ch'êng[1] in Ch'u, and the lord of Yang-ch'êng entrusted him with the defence of his domains, breaking a jade crescent into two halves, one of which he gave to Mêng Shêng, who made 'a solemn undertaking to obey no one who could not produce the other half of the crescent. Shortly afterwards the king[2] of Ch'u died and the officers of Ch'u revolted against the late king's favourite minister Wu Ch'i. An armed rising took place where the dead king lay in state, and in this rising the lord of Yang-ch'êng was involved. He incurred the displeasure of the Ch'u government, and was obliged to flee from his domains, which were at once annexed by Ch'u. 'I have been entrusted by another with the defence of his domains,' said Mêng Shêng, 'and am pledged to yield them only to one who can produce the proper tally. The tally is not forthcoming, but the forces at my disposal are so small that I cannot put up any resistance. Under such circumstances it would be wrong for me to go on living.'

'If your death would be of any advantage to the lord of Yang-ch'êng,' said his disciple Hsü Jo, 'I agree that it would be right for you to die on his behalf. But it would not be of any advantage to him, and would mean the breaking of the Mohist succession. You must not do it.' 'I do not agree with you,' said Mêng Shêng. 'The bond between me and the lord of Yang-ch'êng was a close one. I was not merely his teacher, I was his friend; I was not merely his friend, but also his minister. Were I not to die, from now onwards men seeking a teacher of high principles would certainly not look for him among the Mohists, men seeking a worthy friend would certainly

---

[1] In southern Honan. It was a small independent enclave in Ch'u territory. Such enclaves were often maintained in connection with the cult of some local deity. The Lord of Yang-ch'êng was probably head of the cult of the Yang-ch'êng mountain.

[2] King Tao, in 381 B.C.

not look for him among the Mohists, men seeking a
loyal minister would certainly not look for him among
the Mohists. Whereas by dying I shall not merely be
carrying out the principles of Mohism, but ensuring the
continuance of its mission. I intend to confer the Grand
Mastership upon T'ien Hsiang-tzu, in the land of Sung.
He is well qualified for the position; you need have no
fear about the line of succession being broken.'

'If you are determined to do as you say,' said Hsü Jo,
'I beg to be allowed to die first in order to prepare the
way for you.' And just as Mêng Shêng was about to die
for his lord, so Hsü Jo too died, as forerunner to his
master.[1]

Mêng Shêng then sent two men to hand on the Grand
Mastership to T'ien Hsiang-tzu.

When finally Mêng Shêng killed himself, a hundred
and eighty-three of his followers died with him. The
two who had gone to Sung to confer the succession
upon T'ien Hsiang-tzu wanted to go back and die for
Mêng Shêng in Ch'u. But he would not allow them to.
'Mêng,' he said, 'has now conferred the Grand Mastership on me and I forbid it.' But they disobeyed him,
went to Ch'u and died. Their fellow Mohists, however,
considered that in disobeying the Grand Master, they
had proved themselves unworthy of their mission,[2]
and . . .

'Their Way,' says Chuang Tzu, speaking of the
Mohists, 'is too harsh. It makes of life a sad and
dreary business. Their standard of conduct is impossible to live up to. . . . It is contrary to the heart of

[1] Not 'cut off his own head in front of his master,' as
Wilhelm and Bodde both translate it. It is surely not
very easy to cut off one's own head.

[2] The story ends lamely, but some sentences from another chapter have got mixed with the text, which is
defective. We must supply at the end 'erased their
names from the Mohist records' or the like.

the world, and the world at large could never endure it. Mo Tzu himself may have been capable of bearing such a burden; but who else in all the world?'

This lack of psychological subtlety, this failure to understand 'the heart of the world,' was the main weakness of the Mohists. They did not realize that human nature can perfectly well tolerate contradictory beliefs, can believe simultaneously in Fate and liberty of moral action; they did not realize as the Confucians did that the value of the ritual is not to be measured by utilitarian standards, but is 'something that comes from inside; when the heart is uneasy we support it with ritual.'[1]

But the foregoing pages have surely proved Mencius's 'Mo Tzu wished to reduce mankind to the level of wild beasts,' to be a biassed and intemperate statement.

Mencius's attack on the quasi-Mohist Sung K'êng[2] was based on what can hardly have been other than a wilful misunderstanding of a well-known Mohist term. The Mohists used the word li in the sense 'beneficial' as opposed to 'harmful'; they did not mean by it, as the Confucians did, 'what pays,' as opposed to what is right.[3]

Here is the passage:

When Sung K'êng was on the way to Ch'u, Mencius met him at Shih-ch'iu, and asked him where he was going. 'I hear that Ch'in and Ch'u are at war.' Sung K'êng said, 'and I am going to see the king of Ch'u and

[1] Li Chi, ch. 25.
[2] See The Way and Its Power, p. 90.
[3] Compare the Mohist definition of 'right,' (i), ch. 40, beginning: i li yeh: 'right' is 'what is beneficial.'

persuade him to stop fighting. If I fail with the king of Ch'u, I shall see the king of Ch'in and persuade him to stop. With one or the other of them I am sure to succeed.' 'I am not asking you to tell me anything in detail,' said Mencius, 'but I should like to hear what general line you are going to take. How shall you persuade them?' 'I shall tell them,' said Sung K'êng, 'that this war is not *li*' (i.e. can produce no good results). 'Your intention is admirable,' said Mencius, 'but the term you have chosen is not a proper one. If you convince the two kings, whose hearts are set on gain (*li*), that there is nothing to be gained by this war, they will recall their armies. Thereupon the officers in those armies, delighted at the cessation of hostilities, will henceforward make "gain" their watchword. Those of them who are ministers will think of nothing but gain in serving their prince, at home they will think of nothing but gain in serving their fathers and nothing but gain in serving their elder brothers. Soon prince and ministers, fathers and sons, older and younger brothers will all abandon goodness and duty and think of nothing but gain in their dealings with one another; and ruin will be the inevitable result.'

Mencius goes on, of course, to say that what Sung K'êng ought to have preached to the two kings was 'Goodness and duty,' and he paints a glowing picture of the moral regeneration that will ensue if the kings are converted. Yes, indeed; but the 'if' is a very big one!

We possess no actual specimen of Sung K'êng's writings or speeches, and do not know by what arguments he proved that war 'does not pay.' But there is preserved in the *Chan Kuo T'sê*[1] a description of the economic disadvantage of war which though it is certainly somewhat later than Sung

[1] Ch'i stories, II.

K'êng's time, probably embodies much the same arguments that he and his followers used:

War damages a country and drains the resources of its towns and cities to such an extent that after such damage and waste have occurred a country is seldom fit to take its place among the other States. When a country is at war, the moment that they hear of it the gentry make over their private goods to the military depots and bring all their stocks of wine and food to place at the disposal of the fighting forces. They are ordered to cut up the poles of their carriages to make firewood and to slaughter their cattle to provision the troops, till their houses[1] are stripped bare. Those who are to be left at home betake themselves to prayers and supplications;[2] the prince, to exorcisms and purifications. The cities and small towns set up Holy Places; in the market-towns all business ceases and everyone has to devote himself to the king's service. With the result that the whole land becomes like a desert.

After the battle, when the dead have been buried and the wounded brought home, even if a victory has been won, the costs of the expedition will have exhausted the country and the sounds of wailing and weeping will distress the ruler's heart. The families of those who have fallen will ruin themselves in their desire to give them a worthy burial; the wounded will spend all they possess in order to procure the necessary drugs. Meanwhile those who have returned safe and sound will celebrate their triumph by continual banqueting and carousing, the losses thus incurred being fully equal to those occasioned by death and wounds.

Indeed the losses sustained by the peasants are more than could be made good by ten years' field-work. Moreover during the campaign spears and lances have

[1] Reading uncertain.
[2] Always accompanied by sacrifices.

been broken, rings and bow-strings, cross-bows and chariots smashed or spoilt; horses worn out. More than half of the equipment has been lost or destroyed. Of the arms intended for the troops a great part will either have been privately disposed of by the department in charge of them or hidden by ministers and officials or stolen by lackeys and grooms, the total loss being more than ten years' field-work could make good. No country which has suffered this twofold drain upon its resources can hope to take its place among the other kingdoms.

Or supposing what is undertaken to be the siege of an enemy city. All the people will have to devote themselves to constructing covered chariots and shelters, battering-rams and wheeled towers. The soldiers will have to exist herded together promiscuously while they are boring tunnels. Thus those at home are worn out with carpentering and metalwork, the men in the field with tunnelling and burrowing. A general who without doffing armour for a month or even several months can capture a city is thought to have done quick work. By this time the superiors are tired of training men; the troops themselves have had enough of war. Hence it seldom happens that an army which has secured the surrender of as many as three cities is able to secure a real victory over the enemy.

Therefore I say, 'War and conquest should not be made the first objects in a State.'

Mencius and the Agriculturalists

A man named Hsü Hsing, who professed allegiance to the teachings of Shên Nung,[1] came from Ch'u to T'êng. Having obtained an audience with duke Wên of

[1] The Holy Farmer, patron deity of agriculture.

T'êng[1] he said to him, 'My lord, I have come from distant parts because I heard that you were practising Government by Goodness. I want to be given a plot of land and become your subject.' The duke gave him somewhere to live, and he settled there with thirty or forty disciples. They all wore clothes made out of dolicho-fibre, and were capable of supporting themselves by making hemp-sandals and weaving mats.

Now it happened that at this time Ch'ên Hsiang and his younger brother Ch'ên Hsin, Confucians who were followers of Ch'ên Liang,[2] arrived from Sung with their ploughs on their backs, saying: 'It is said that a ruler who puts into practice the Government of the Sages is himself a Sage, and we should like to be subjects of a Sage.'

The elder brother Ch'ên Hsiang presently met Hsü Hsing and was so favourably impressed by him that he entirely abandoned Confucianism, and became a pupil of Hsü Hsing. Ch'ên Hsiang also met Mencius. 'My new master,' he said, 'admits that the lord of T'êng is indeed better than most rulers, but says that all the same he is ignorant of the true Way. A sovereign, he says, ought to get his food by tilling the soil side by side with his subjects and take his morning and evening meal along with them, while at the same time attending to government. But T'êng has its royal granaries and stores, its treasury and arsenal, which means that the prince lives by imposing upon his subjects and cannot really be called a good ruler.' . . . 'Does Hsü Hsing wear a hat?' asked Mencius. 'Yes, he does,' said Ch'ên Hsiang. 'What is it made of?' asked Mencius. 'Of plain silk,' said Ch'ên Hsiang. 'Does he weave the silk himself?' asked Mencius. 'No,' said Ch'ên Hsiang, 'he gets it by giving grain in exchange.' 'Why does he not weave it himself?' asked Mencius. 'Because,' said Ch'ên Hsiang, 'that would in-

[1] See above, p. 92.

[2] A distinguished Confucian from Ch'u, who had studied Confucianism in the north.

terfere with his farming.' 'Does he cook in metal pots and earthenware pans, and does he plough with an iron share?' asked Mencius. 'He does,' replied Ch'ên Hsiang. 'Does he make them himself?' asked Mencius. 'No,' said Ch'en Hsiang. 'He gets them by giving grain in exchange.' 'He does not then consider,' said Mencius, 'that by getting tools and utensils in exchange for grain he is imposing upon the potter and the metal-worker. And it is equally certain that the potter and metal-worker, when they take grain in exchange for tools and utensils, are not imposing upon the farmer.

'After all, why is it that Hsü Hsing does not do his own potting and metal-work, and instead of making in his own house everything that he needs, goes through all the complicated business of bartering with this craftsman and that? Surely he might spare himself all this trouble?'

'The reason is,' said Ch'ên Hsiang, 'that if he carried on the business of every kind of craftsman, he would have no time left to till the soil.' 'Why then should you think,' said Mencius, 'that someone who is carrying on the government of a kingdom has time also to till the soil? The truth is, that some kinds of business are proper to the great and others to the small. Even supposing each man could unite in himself all the various kinds of skill required in every craft, if he had to make for himself everything that he used, this would merely lead to everyone being completely prostrate with fatigue. True indeed is the saying, "Some work with their minds, others with their bodies. Those who work with their minds rule, while those who work with their bodies are ruled. Those who are ruled produce food; those who rule are fed." That this is right is universally recognized everywhere under Heaven.'

'One of Hsü Hsing's principles,' said Ch'ên Hsiang, 'is that if in the market there were no difference of price according to the quality of the articles, then there would be no cheating. You could send a half-grown boy to market, and no one could possibly deceive him. A length of cloth would cost exactly the same as an equal length of silk. A bundle of hemp-thread and a bundle of silk floss that weighed the same would be sold at the same price. And so with grain of whatever kind and shoes of the same size, irrespective of their quality.'

'It is a fact about things,' said Mencius, 'that they differ greatly in quality; some are twice as good as others, some five times, ten times or a hundred times, some a thousand, ten thousand times. If you attempt to put them all on the same level, this can only lead to general confusion. If coarse shoes and fine shoes cost the same who is going to make fine shoes?[1] If this idea of Hsü Hsing's were adopted, it would merely induce people to practise deceit. How could a State possibly be governed upon such a principle?'

We have seen that Mencius had a habit of parodying the views of those with whom he disagreed. We cannot be confident that Hsü Hsing would have accepted the above account as a true description of his views or of the arguments by which he defended them. But several points of interest emerge from the narrative. We see how Government by Goodness was actually supposed to work, that is to say, to establish its ascendancy over all China. The agricultural population was still in a very mobile condition, and it was conceived of as possible that workers should drift away from an oppressive country to one where conditions were more to their liking; moreover, there was still free land waiting to be cultivated. If this process of migration went far enough, the bad States would ultimately be depopulated and the good State would become so strong in numbers that it would dominate the whole of China.

[1] For gentlemen to wear.

Ch'ên Chung

Mencius does not mention Chuang Tzu, who was his contemporary. Taoism, under that name, he could not mention, for the term was not invented till long after his time. But he twice attacks a certain Ch'ên Chung of Ch'i who disavowed 'the duties of kinship, the loyalty of minister to prince and of inferior to superior,' and rather than take service with a government of which he disapproved, endured a life of extreme hardship and poverty. What Ch'ên Chung's metaphysical views were we are not told. There is no reason to suppose that they were similar to those of the Taoists. But in his refusal to enter public service and his denial of all social obligations he reminds us strongly of the Taoist recluses who figure in *Chuang Tzu*.

Ch'ên Chung, who seems to have been still alive in 298 B.C.,[1] belonged to an important family in the land of Ch'i. 'His ancestors had held high office for many generations on end, and his elder brother held a fief from which he received a revenue of 10,000 chung.'[2] As it was against Ch'ên Chung's principles to live on what he regarded as ill-gotten gains, he left his brother's house and set up at a remote place called Wu-ling. Here he supported himself by making hemp-sandals, his wife twisting the hemp-thread. Their livelihood was very precarious and on one occasion Ch'ên had nothing to eat

[1] See *Chan Kuo Ts'ê*, Ch'i stories, **IV**.
[2] A tenth of the revenue of a prime minister.

for three days. 'His ears no longer heard, his eyes no longer saw.' But he knew that on a tree by the well-side there was a plum, half eaten by maggots. In desperation he groped his way to the spot, gulped the plum down, and so recovered his sight and hearing.

Once when he was staying for a while at his brother's house someone sent the family a live goose as a present. 'What use can they suppose you could make of a cackling thing like that?' Ch'ên Chung asked, frowning. A few days later his mother killed the goose and not telling him what it was gave him some for his dinner. 'I suppose you know what it is you are eating,' said his brother, coming into the room. 'That's cackle-cackle's flesh!' Ch'ên went out into the courtyard and vomited.

We might be tempted to think that Ch'ên Chung was, among his other scrupulosities, a vegetarian. But I do not think that is the point of the story. He regarded the goose, which was no doubt a gift from one of the tenants, as part of his brother's ill-gotten gains; hence his disapproval of the arrival of 'cackle-cackle' and his nausea at the thought of having partaken of such a dish.[1]

'Everyone believed,' says Mencius elsewhere, 'that Ch'ên Chung would have refused the kingdom of Ch'i, had it been offered to him, rather than violate his principles. But his were merely the sort of scruples that make a man refuse a bowl of rice or a dish of soup. When it came to things of the greatest importance to man, the duties of kinship, the loyalty of minister to prince, or inferior to superior— these he swept away. To infer that because he was scrupulous when little was at stake he could be relied

[1] See *The Way and Its Power*, p. 38.

upon when great things were at stake, was quite un-justified.'

Mencius, as we have seen, did not spare his op-ponents while they remained in opposition. But as soon as they admitted their errors, bygones were to be bygones; they were to be received into the Confucian school without question or reproach.

'Those who flee from Mo invariably betake them-selves to Yang, and those who flee from Yang come with equal certainty to Confucianism. When they come, they should be received without further to-do. Nowadays those who carry on controversies with the followers of Yang and Mo treat them as one does a stray pig. Not content with having chivied them back into the sty, they must needs proceed to tie them by the leg.'

Mencius and the Disciples

We have seen that Mencius demanded much from his patrons; the following story shows that towards his disciples he was no less exacting. Yo-chêng K'o, a disciple who lived in Lu (the home of Confucius), joined the cortège of Wang Huan, a Ch'i general who had been on a mission in Lu. The day after his arrival in Ch'i, Yo-chêng K'o came to visit Mencius, who was then living in Ch'i. 'So you have come to see me after all!' said Mencius. 'Why should you say that?' asked Yo-chêng K'o. 'How many days have you been here?' asked Mencius in return. 'I arrived last night,' said Yo-chêng. 'Last night!' said Mencius. 'If you arrived last night, you cannot com-

plain of my speaking as I did.' 'I had to arrange first
about a lodging,' said Yo-chêng. 'And has anyone
ever taught you,' asked Mencius, 'that a disciple ought
first to arrange about his lodging, and then come to
see his master?' 'I did wrong,' said Yo-chêng. 'What
induced you to travel in the cortège of Wang Huan,'
continued Mencius, 'was the food and drink. I should
never have suspected that one who was versed in the
Way of the Ancients would be lured by food and
drink.'

Methods of Argument

Mencius tells us that he did not like arguing, and
was only driven to do so in order to save the world
from dangerous heresies. Thus like the Mohists who
elaborated a system of defensive argument (just as
they developed a special theory of military defence),
Mencius was driven by the increasing activity of his
opponents into self-protective controversies, in which
he would have been utterly routed, had not his enemies been as feeble in argument as he was. It was
as a teacher, depending upon the appeal of vivid incitement, rising sometimes (as in the Bull Mountain
allegory) to methods very near to those of poetry,
that Mencius excelled. As a controversialist he is
nugatory. The whole discussion (Book VI) about
whether Goodness and Duty are internal or external
is a mass of irrelevant analogies, most of which could
equally well be used to disprove what they are intended to prove. In other passages, the analogy gets
mixed up with the actual point at issue. A glaring

example is the discussion (IV.1.XVII) with Shun-
yü K'un, who was shocked by Mencius's reluctance
to take office. Shun-yü K'un's argument is as follows:
just as in a case of great urgency (despite the taboo
on men and women touching hands) a man will give
his hand to his sister-in-law to save her from drowning; so in the present emergency of China you ought
to put aside the general principles that make you
hesitate to take office, and place yourself at the disposal of the government. Mencius's reply is: 'When
the world is drowning, it can only be rescued by
the Way (of the Former Kings); when a sister-in-law
is drowning, she can be rescued with the hand. Do
you want me to rescue the world with my hand?'

This is at best a very cheap debating point. The
proper answer (which may or may not have been
made, but does not occur in *Mencius*) of course is,
'Figuratively, yes. Just as one breaks taboos in an
emergency and gives a hand to someone in peril, so
I want you in the present political emergency to
sacrifice your principles and "give a hand" to public
affairs.'

It will be remembered that at the time of the
annexation of Yen by Ch'i, Mencius prophesied that
unless the conquered people were treated better than
their former rulers had treated them, Yen would not
long remain subject. In 312 B.C.[1] Yen revolted. 'I do
not know how I shall face Mencius,' said the king
of Ch'i.

This is the latest mention of Mencius that can be
dated with certainty. In most Chinese works of reference it is stated that he died in 289 B.C. at the
age of eighty-three, but there is no real evidence
for this. The book *Mencius* had to wait a long time

[1] Possibly earlier. See above, p. 62.

for its canonization. Even as late as the 7th century A.D. Lu Tê-ming, in his series of phonetic glosses on the Classics, includes *Chuang Tzu*, but omits *Mencius*, which was classified merely as a philosophic book till the 12th century. Then it became a Classic (a scripture, as we should say), the interpretation of which remained under official control till recent times.

The
Realists

The people whom I call the Realists are called in Chinese the *Fa Chia*, School of Law, because they held that law should replace morality. But hand in hand with their reliance on law, on punishments and rewards, went a number of other demands, summed up in the principle that government must be based upon 'the actual facts of the world as it now exists.'[1] They rejected all appeals to tradition, all reliance on supernatural sanctions and trust in supernatural guidance. For this reason the term 'Realist' seems to me to fit the general tendency of their beliefs better than 'School of Law,' which only indicates one aspect of their teaching. We might, if we wanted a narrower term, as an alternative to 'School of Law' call them the Amoralists.

Naturally the doctrine of the Realists was not an entirely new creation. We find when we come to examine it that it had, strangely enough, a good deal in common with Taoism, and stranger still, despite its bellicosity and amoralism, with the pacifist and profoundly moral doctrines of the Mohists. Fundamental to Realism was the rejection of private standards of right and wrong. 'Right' to them meant 'what the rulers want,' 'wrong' meant what the rulers do not want. No individual or school of thought must be allowed to set up any other standard or ideal.

[1] *Han Fei Tzu*, 46, p. 37.

We find much the same demand in Mo Tzu:[1]
long ago when the people first came into being, each
person had his own private standard of right and
wrong. This became so inconvenient that the people
set up rulers who gave out that 'what those above
consider right, you are all to consider right; what
those above consider wrong, you are all to consider
wrong.' But whereas the Realist ruler decided for
himself on grounds of expediency what is to be regarded as right and wrong, the Mohist ruler, no less
than his subjects, conforms to what is above him,
conforms that is to say to the Will of Heaven, so
that in fact it is Heaven and not merely the ruler
that the people are called upon to obey.

Again, there is in Mohism a tendency to carry
principles to their logical conclusion, without the
mitigation of customary scruples and compunctions.
We have seen this in relation to the traditional rules
of warfare.[2] If in the passage quoted above we were
to substitute 'then frontiers will not be extended'
for 'then the violent will escape punishment,' the
whole passage might easily be an extract from Realist
writings. The ruthlessness of Shang Tzu[3] does in fact
find certain anticipations in Mohism.

One of the principles of Realist government was
mutual espionage. The people were to be organized
into groups 'who were mutually responsible for each
other and were obliged to denounce each other's
crimes.'[4] A member of the group who failed to do
this was to be punished as though he had himself
committed the crime. We find something not unlike

[1] Chaps. XI–XIII.
[2] See above, p. 131.
[3] See below, p. 202.
[4] The Book of Lord Shang, p. 58.

this in Mo Tzu:[1] Anyone who discovers that somebody is doing good service to his country must report
the fact to the authorities and will be rewarded as
though he himself had performed the service; but
anyone who finds that somebody is doing harm to
his country must report the fact, and if he fails to do
so, he will be punished as though he himself were
guilty of the crime. Finally, the attitude of Mohists
and Realists towards magic and ritual was much the
same. Both condemned them as unprofitable, the
Mohists chiefly because they are expensive and waste-
ful; the Realists because they do not increase the
military power of the State.

By what I have said above I do not mean to imply
that Realism was directly derived from Mohism or
that any particular contact existed between the two
schools; but only that some part of the stern Realist
outlook is already to be found where we should least
expect it—in the works of the pacifist and humanitarian Mo Tzu.

With Taoism, on the other hand, Realism has a
very real and close connection. Both doctrines reject
the appeal to tradition, to the 'Way of the Former
Kings,' upon which the whole curriculum of the
Confucians was based. Both regard the logicians
(such as Hui Tzu and Kung-sun Lung) as hair-
splitting sophists, both condemn book learning and
would have the people kept 'dull and stupid,' incuri-
ous of all that lies beyond their own village and
home. Even the mystical doctrine of wu-wei, the
Non-activity of the ruler by which everything is
activated, finds a non-mystical counterpart in Realism. When every requirement of the ruler has been
embodied in law and the penalties for disobedience

[1] Ch. XIII.

have been made so heavy that no one dares to incur them, the Realist ruler can sink deep into his cushions and enjoy himself;[1] 'everything' (just as in Taoism) 'will happen of its own accord.'

Both *Han Fei Tzu* and *Kuan Tzu*, the two main collections of Realist writings that we still possess, contain sections that are purely Taoist. I shall deal with this point later, in discussing the life of Han Fei. Here I will only mention that while other ways of thought are repeatedly and bitterly condemned by the Realists, Taoism comes off very lightly, and is indeed only directly attacked in one passage: 'there are some whom the world regards as heroes because they chose to leave the throng and walk alone, who pride themselves on being different from other men, who accept the doctrines of quietism and compose sayings that are vague and mysterious. Your servant submits that quietism is a useless teaching and that sayings vague and mysterious are inimical to Law. Sayings that in their upshot are inimical to Law and teachings that in their upshot are of no utility, the world regards as enlightened. My opinion, on the other hand, is that a man is born to serve his prince and nourish his parents, for which purposes quietism is of no use; man is born to discuss loyalty, good faith, law and the art of ruling, for which purpose vague and mysterious sayings will not stand him in good stead. For which reason I say that such sayings and the doctrine of quietism belong to a way of thought that can only lead the world astray.'[2]

With the Confucianism of Mencius Realism has nothing in common at all, such is the gulf that separates Government by Goodness from Government by

[1] See *Shang Tzu*, 18, p. 120.

[2] *Han Fei Tzu*, 51.

Law. The Realist 'does not prize morality; he prizes Law.'[1] He knows that Goodness (*jên*) alone does not enable a father to keep unruly children in order; still less can it enable a ruler to govern a mass of people to whom he is bound by no ties of kinship. Force can always secure obedience; an appeal to morality, very seldom.[2]

But with the Confucianism of Hsün Tzu, who flourished about the middle of the 3rd century B.C.[3] Realism had much in common. This is not surprising; for it was from Hsün Tzu that Han Fei Tzu received his early training. To give a complete account of Hsün Tzu's doctrines would be to go far beyond the intended scope of this book. I will here only discuss the chief ways in which he differs from his predecessor Mencius.

To begin with, though he accepts the main features of Government by Goodness as practised by the True Kings, he lays stress on the importance of 'punishments and rewards' to an extent which would have horrified Mencius. Again, Mencius insisted upon using common words in a way that was at variance with their ordinary and accepted meanings or, in the case of words that had several accepted meanings, upon arbitrarily accepting one meaning and rejecting another. For example, *hsing* (nature) meant in ordinary parlance the qualities that a thing has to start with. Mencius insisted upon using the word *hsing* in a special sense that was quite at variance with its ordinary and accepted meaning. He

[1] *Shang Tzu*, p. 121.

[2] *Han Fei Tzu*, 49.

[3] If we accept as history all the anecdotes in which he figures, he must have lived from c. 335 till 213 B.C., that is to say, 122 years, which is unlikely.

meant by it the feelings of right and wrong, which according to him were inborn. Thus if a man showed deference to his elder brother, it was not because those in charge of his education had taught him to do so, but because an inborn sense of right and wrong prompted him to deference of this kind.

✳   Hsün Tzu, on the other hand, believed that ethical standards were acquired from environment, and that to use the word 'nature' as a way of alluding to them was at variance with 'common parlance as it exists among men.'[1] According to him man comes into the world not with a ready-made ethical standard, but with a set of full-blown passions and desires, such as love, hate, joy, grief, anger and so on. If all of these are given full play, the result can only be universal violence and confusion. In this sense man's natural propensities are bad, whereas according to Mencius they are good.

Again, the word *li*, 'profit,' had in ordinary parlance two meanings, easily distinguishable according to context. It meant in some contexts material gain as opposed to ethical aims, opportunism as opposed to moral conduct; in others, the 'profitable' as opposed to the 'harmful.' Mencius flew in the face of common parlance by refusing ever to understand the term except in the first sense. Hsün Tzu, without any loss of clarity, uses it now in one sense, now in the other. Between the time of Mencius and that of Hsün Tzu's maturity a great deal of thought had been given in China to the question of language and its relation to reality.[2] The importance of these studies to the Realist is obvious; for if the whole of behaviour is to be regulated by Law, the ruler must have at

[1] *Hsün Tzu*, XXII, beginning.
[2] See *The Way and Its Power*, p. 59.

his disposal 'good words' with which to formulate these laws. The language of law must be 'succinct, easily understood and consistent.' In cases where words have several meanings it is a waste of time to discuss which of those meanings is 'right,' as though it were a moral question, or which is 'true.' The ruler must define by statute the sense in which he wishes them to be understood, and in course of time these meanings will be popularly accepted as 'right' and 'true.'

Names should correspond to realities; but the idea that the same name should always be used in speaking of the same reality is a fallacy. In contexts where a single term is not sufficient to make one's meaning clear, one must use a double term.[1] For example, the same horse will sometimes be referred to simply as a 'horse,' sometimes, if clarity demands it, as a 'white horse.' The days were over when the conundrum 'Is a white horse a horse?' bewildered the thinkers of China.

Almost all writers of the period were to some extent influenced by Taoism. Hsün Tzu's twenty-first chapter, the genuineness of which I see no reason to doubt, contains a long mystical section about 'the heart,' which is typically Quietist. It is not therefore surprising to find that his pupil Han Fei Tzu, 'though chiefly interested in the study of language in relation to punishments, in Law and in the art of ruling, based his doctrines upon Lao Tzu and Huang Ti,'[2] that is to say, upon what was later called Taoism. This is borne out by the fact that *Han Fei Tzu* contains several chapters in which a small amount of Realism is diluted with a strong

[1] *Hsün Tzu*, XXII, p. 315.

[2] *Shih Chi*, 63.

dose of Taoism. People who like everything to be neatly pigeon-holed say that these chapters are not genuine, because Han Fei Tzu was a Realist and not a Taoist. But Mencius was a Confucian and not a Taoist; yet he was capable of saying 'All the ten thousand things are complete in me.' Taoism was in the air and every writer was liable to be affected by it.

Two chapters of *Han Fei Tzu*, now generally dismissed as spurious, are entitled 'Explanations of Lao Tzu' and 'Illustrations of Lao Tzu.' They represent an attempt to explain and illustrate the *Tao Te Ching* from a point of view which is sometimes (for example, the second paragraph, on Goodness) purely Confucian, sometimes markedly Realist, sometimes merely utilitarian from a 'common sense' point of view. Seldom is the text allowed to mean what the author meant by it. Whether Han Fei Tzu wrote these chapters or not, it is certainly possible to imagine them being produced by a Realist trained in Confucianism, who under the influence of the times felt a necessity to bring his doctrines by hook or crook into conformity with Taoism.

The Realist Conception of Law

Everyone who does what the State wants is to be rewarded; everyone who does what the State dislikes is to be punished. This principle may seem to us natural and even commonplace; but it was at variance both with the traditional practice of early times and with the ideals of the Confucian period. For example, as regards rewards: over and over again in

the early Chou bronze inscriptions we find rewards
and privileges being given 'because your ancestor
supported the House of Chou,' 'because your father
enjoyed this privilege,' and not because of any actual
services of the man himself. We find both Confucians
and Mohists demanding that people of 'superior
moral character' (hsien) should be rewarded and
put in power, irrespective of their previous achievements. While as regards punishments, not only were
members of a ruling family to a large extent tradition-
ally immune, but also the higher ministers and officials.

If the whole conduct of everyone in the State was
to be controlled by Law, the code of laws must necessarily be extremely lengthy and detailed. They could
not consist, as earlier attempts at codification had
done, of a few general commandments inscribed, in
order to give them supernatural validity, upon sacri-
ficial tripods. 'If their text-book is too summary,'
says Han Fei Tzu,[1] 'pupils will be able to twist
its meaning; if a law is too concise the common
people dispute its intentions. A wise man when he
writes a book sets forth his arguments fully and
clearly; an enlightened ruler, when he makes his laws,
sees to it that every contingency is provided for in
detail.' Not only must the laws be very detailed,
but the penalties[2] enacted in them must be very
heavy: 'Scholars (i.e. Confucians and Mohists) are
always telling us that punishments should be light.
This is the way to bring about confusion and ruin.
The object of rewards is to encourage; that of punishments, to prevent. If rewards are high, then what

[1] 47, p. 43.
[2] The Realist has in mind repressive rather than contrac-
tual law.

the ruler wants will be quickly effected; if punishments are heavy, what he does not want will be swiftly prevented.'[1] Indeed, if punishments are sufficiently heavy, no one will dare to transgress the law: 'the ultimate goal of penalties is that there should be no penalties.'[2]

Even the idea of inscribing laws on tripods and setting them up in the Ancestral Temple shocked the Confucians, who regarded themselves as the sole authentic transmitters of the 'ways of Chou' and claimed the right to teach and interpret these ways to the ruling classes. To the Realists the essence of law was that it should be universally known and understood, 'set forth in documents, supplied to every government office, and distributed among all the people.'[3]

By law and its sanctions an average ruler can keep order among an average people. It may be that once in a thousand generations a ruler appears who can dispense with these instruments. But to tell the people of the present age that they must wait for another Yao or Shun 'is like telling a man who is drowning in Middle China to wait till an expert swimmer arrives from Yüeh.'[4] Similarly it may be that among thousands of people one or two are as honest as the legendary Wei-shêng Kao, but this does not do away with the need for tallies, which were invented not to control the Wei-shêng Kaos, but to frustrate the dishonesty of ordinary people. In the same way, though certain exceptional people might

[1] *Han Fei Tzu*, 46, p. 36.
[2] *Shang Tzu*, 17, p. 105.
[3] *Han Fei Tzu*, 39, p. 9.
[4] *Han Fei Tzu*, 40, p. 17.

be successfully ruled by kindness, the average man cannot be controlled except by law.

The People and the Law

What prevents the people spontaneously falling in with the ruler's plans, is that he takes a long view, whereas they take a short one. He knows that by sacrificing every other activity to food-production and preparation for war a State can become so strong that 'at every battle it will overthrow the enemy's army, at every attack capture a walled city,'[1] and at last secure complete submission on every hand. Then, as in the days of King Wu's victory over the Shang, a period of universal peace will set in, all weapons will be stored away, all warlike activity cease.

The ruler's subjects, on the other hand, are incapable of taking long views. What they hate is toil and danger, what they want is immediate ease and peace, and they are too stupid to see that ultimate safety can only be secured by immediate discomfort and danger. If the ruler pesters them with laws and regulations and threatens them with terrifying penalties, this is with the object of 'saving mankind from disorder and averting the calamities that hang over the whole world, preventing the strong from oppressing the weak, the many from tyrannizing over the few, enabling the old and decrepit to round off their days and the young orphan to grow up to manhood, ensuring that frontiers are not violated and that the horrors of slaughter and captivity are avoided.' No

[1] Shang Tzu, 17, p. 106.

greater service to the people could be imagined; but there are some so stupid as not to realize this and to insist upon regarding the ruler's measures as tyranny. These stupid critics want order to exist in the State, but are opposed to every measure that is calculated to produce order; they all hate insecurity, yet advocate every course that is calculated to produce insecurity. How do I prove this? Severe laws and heavy punishments are what the people hate; but they are the only means by which order can prevail. Compassion and sympathy on the part of the ruler towards his subjects are what the people approve of; but it is through these that a country falls into danger. 'In fact a wise ruler when he makes his laws is bound to find himself in conflict with the world.'[1]

The people are no more capable of understanding the ultimate object of all the unpleasant things that are done to them than a baby is capable of understanding why its head is shaved or its boil lanced. 'If the baby's head is not shaved, there is a return of its malady; if a boil is not lanced, it will go on growing. But while such things are being done to it, though someone holds it close and soothes it and its own mother lovingly performs these operations, the child will nevertheless scream and howl the whole while, not understanding at all that the small pain to which it is being subjected will result in a great gain.'[2]

Those who are in favour of giving the people what they want and saving them from what they dislike are in these days called moral men; whereas those who are in favour of giving the people what they dislike

[1] *Han Fei Tzu*, 14, p. 69.
[2] *Han Fei Tzu*, 50, p. 68.

and interfering with their pleasures are called immoral men. The facts are just the other way round,
and the matter deserves close attention. If the people
are allowed their pleasures, they will soon be suffering
from the pains they most dread; whereas if they are
given what they dread, they will ultimately enjoy the
pleasures that they most covet. Thus what the world
calls 'moral' is in point of fact mere cruelty. Therefore he who rules the people must do so by means
that they dislike; in which case they will end by
getting what they like. Whereas if he uses means
that they like, they will soon have all the evils that
they dread.[1]

All talk of 'giving the people what they want' is
senseless because there is no limit to what they want.
Everyone would be the Son of Heaven if he could.
'Lao Tzu has a saying: "he who knows how to be
content with what he has got can never be despoiled,
he who knows when to stop can never be in peril." It
may be that Lao Tzu himself was deterred by
thoughts of danger and despoilment from seeking to
get more than he should have been content with.
But to suppose that ordinary people can be kept in
order by giving them a sufficiency is to imagine that
they are all on a par with Lao Tzu.'[2]

Smith and Wesson

'If it is a name it should mean just that thing, it
should mean a revolver, and not a person; but it

[1] *Shang Tzu*, 7, pp. 59 and 60.
[2] *Han Fei Tzu*, 46, p. 38.

would not mean a revolver if it had not already meant a person. Well, well.'[1] That the name of a person should come to be the name of a revolver may possibly be distressing to the human bearers of the name, but it does not disorganize the State. In countless instances, however, according to Han Fei Tzu, good names are popularly given to socially harmful people, with the result that the efficiency and security of the State are gravely impaired. For example, 'those who further the private interests of old friends are called "staunch," those who distribute largesses out of the public funds are called "kind men," those who do not care for emoluments and value only themselves are called "gentlemen," those who twist the law in favour of their relations are called "men of principle." Those who do not support officials but favour their own associates are called "free lances" . . .'[2] and so on through an endless list of misnomers. The formula is indeed repeated in different forms so often in *Han Fei Tzu* that it becomes tedious. In order to understand the author's insistence upon the point we must remember that the Confucians, Mohists and other schools of thought actually used these vague terms of moral approbation (superior, loyal, good, wise and so on) to designate those whom the State ought to put in authority; whereas according to the Realists the only qualification for a task was proved capacity to do it efficiently.

In Realist writings that can be accepted as belonging to this period there is no such searching analysis of language in relation to law as we find in *Hsün Tzu*. Moreover Hsün Tzu assumes that it is possible to frame laws in language that is intelligible to every-

[1] Gertrude Stein in *Everybody's Autobiography*.
[2] *Han Fei Tzu*, 47.

body. One Realist essay,[1] however, asserts that laws cannot be understood without official explanation any more than ancient literary texts can be understood apart from their traditional glosses: 'The language used in books made by wise men of former times cannot be understood by those to whom these works are handed down in after ages unless it is explained by a teacher. Anyone who studies them without a teacher, trying to discover what they mean merely by the use of his own intelligence, will not till his dying day make out either the words or the general meaning. In the same way, it is necessary for the wise ruler to set up offices and appoint officials to deal with laws and decrees, who are to act as teachers of the general public, that there may be no doubt as to the precise meaning of terms.'

Throughout the later history of China decrees were formulated in literary language and it was the duty of local officials to explain them in the vernacular. The sole exception was the Mongol dynasty; and this was not due to any democratic theory, but to the fact that, at any rate at the beginning of the dynasty, the Mongols themselves did not understand literary Chinese.

Agriculture and War

The sole aim of a State is to maintain and if possible to expand its frontiers. Food-production and military preparations are the only activities which the State should support; the agricultural labourer and the

[1] *Shang Tzu*, 26, p. 163.

soldier, the only classes of citizen that it should honour and encourage. Unfortunately agriculture is toilsome and war dangerous, whereas what the people want is ease and safety. Fortunately, however, they also covet gain while they are alive and long for fame after they are dead, and by taking these two factors into due account the ruler can induce them to endure the toil from which they shrink and face the dangers that they dread. 'If there is no hope of gain except from the soil, the people will work hard in their fields; if there is no hope of fame except through services in warfare, the people will be ready to lay down their lives. If at home they work to their uttermost, then land will not be left uncultivated; if abroad they are ready to lay down their lives, then the enemy will be defeated. If the enemy is defeated and land is not left uncultivated, then without more ado a country becomes rich and strong.'[1] 'Following the way of the world, rulers of today neglect the law-abiding and give scope to the argumentative and clever, keep back the efficient and strong and advance the moral and good; consequently the common people do not put their energy into ploughing and fighting.

'Now when the people do not exert themselves to the utmost in their fields, food supplies run short at home; and when they do not do their whole duty in battle, the striking power of the State becomes weak abroad. Under these circumstances even a country with ten thousand leagues of territory and an army of a million men is as defenceless as a single individual standing alone in the middle of a flat plain.

'Now, former kings were able to make their people tread on naked swords, face showers of arrows and stones. Was it that the people liked doing it? Not

[1] *Shang Tzu*, 6, p. 50.

at all; but they had learnt that by doing so they escaped from even worse harm. Therefore I would have the people told that if they want gain, it is only by ploughing that they can get it; if they fear harm, it will only be by fighting that they can escape it. Then everyone within the borders of the land would know that he could get no happiness without first applying himself to ploughing and warfare. The country might be small, but the grain produced would be much; the inhabitants might be few, but their military power would be great. A country that devoted itself to these two ends would not have to wait long before it established hegemony or even complete mastery over all other States.'[1] Mencius advocated various traditional forms of co-operative agriculture and condemned those who thought only of *jên t'u*, 'getting the most out of the soil.' It is clear that this latter principle was the one followed by the Realists. They were for sweeping away all the old agricultural customs and conventions that hindered maximum production. But the exact nature of the reforms they demanded is very obscure. About warfare the texts are far more explicit. The whole population is to be divided into three armies, the first consisting of able-bodied men, the second of able-bodied women, the third of the old and weak of both sexes. The three armies are to be kept strictly apart. The second and third armies are to be used when defending a besieged town; only the first goes into the open field.

It is a misfortune for a prosperous country not to be at war; for in peace time it will breed 'the Six Maggots, to wit, Rites and Music, the Songs and the

[1] *Shang Tzu*, 25, p. 155.

Book,[1] the cultivation of goodness, filial piety and respect for elders, sincerity and truth, purity and integrity, kindness and morality, detraction of warfare and shame at taking part in it. In a country which has these twelve things, the ruler will not promote agriculture and warfare, with the result that he will become impoverished and his territory diminished.'[2]

'Concentrate the people upon warfare, and they will be brave; let them care about other things, and they will be cowardly. . . . A people that looks to warfare as a ravening wolf looks at a piece of meat is a people that can be used. In general, fighting is a thing that the people detest. A ruler who can make the people delight in war will become king of kings. In a country that is really strong the father will send his son, the elder brother his younger brother, the wife her husband, all saying as they speed him: "Conquer, or let me never see you again." '[3]

'If the only gate to riches and honour is battle, then when the people hear that there is war they will congratulate one another; at home and in the streets, at their eating and at their drinking, all the songs they sing will be of war.'[4]

'How to get the people to die' is a problem that continually occupies the Realists. We have seen various methods, such as an appeal to their cupidity or the knowledge that the utmost horrors of battle are as nothing compared with the fate that awaits the coward when the battle is done. Mencius had

[1] The Book of History.
[2] Shang Tzu, 13, p. 87.
[3] Shang Tzu, 18, p. 116.
[4] Shang Tzu, 17, p. 111.

quite other views on this subject, as is shown in the
following passage:

There had been a skirmish between Tsou and Lu.
'I lost thirty-three officers,' said duke Mu[1] to Mencius,
'and of the commoners present not one died in their
defence. If I kill them for their treachery it means
executing a huge number of people. On the other hand,
if I do not execute them, I shall be sparing men who
watched their superiors being slaughtered and did nothing to help them. What am I to do?'
'In times of trouble or when there is famine in the
land,' said Mencius, 'the old and feeble among your
people drop by the wayside and are rolled into the
nearest ditch, while the able-bodied escape some this
way, some that, drifting off in their thousands;[2] yet all
the while your own granaries are full, your own treasuries
well stocked, and none of your officials tell you what is
going on. Such is the suffering that the negligence of
those above can inflict upon those below.
'Master Tsêng said, "Beware, beware! what goes
out from you will come back to you." If now or here-
after the people get a chance to pay back the wrongs
that are done to them, do not blame them, my lord.
Were you to adopt Government by Goodness, then the
people would feel kinship with those above them and
lay down their lives for their officers.' (Mencius, I. 2,
xii.)

[1] Legge (p. 393) assumes that this duke Mu was Mu of
Lu. But duke Mu of Lu died before Mencius was born,
or at any rate while he was still a child. Duke Mu of
Tsou is meant.
[2] Compare above, p. 112.

Classes to Be Eliminated

These are so numerous that it will be convenient to take them alphabetically, beginning with aristocrats. There are no hereditary privileges; all preferment is gained by distinction in war. The aristocracy therefore automatically disappears. But it never seems to have struck the Realists that hereditary kingship was a very odd anomaly to leave untouched in a system that purported to abolish hereditary privileges and prided itself upon ruthless logic. Other classes singled out for particular attack were artistans, hermits, innkeepers, merchants, moralists, philanthropists, scholars, soothsayers and swashbucklers. A word or two of explanation is needed in each case.

The artisans intended are workers in luxury crafts such as makers of fine tissues, brocades and embroideries, carvers and painters. Hermits we have met with frequently in *Chuang Tzu*. 'They live in inaccessible caves, pretending to be engaged in deep cogitation. The greater among them abuse the ways of the world; the humbler mislead the people.' Innkeepers must be abolished because people who travel are apt to be 'troublesome, false, restless, and engaged in secret plots.' 'If travellers had nowhere to eat they would be obliged to betake themselves to agriculture, and land at present uncultivated would be tilled.'[1]

Merchants had already been attacked by Hsün Tzu.[2] They were a relatively new class, and appeared

[1] *Shang Tzu*, 2, p. 11.
[2] XII, p. 168.

to exist merely in order to create artificial scarcities.
Popular ideas about the power and wickedness of
merchants are well illustrated by the romantic story
of Lü Pu-wei, as it is told in the Shih Chi.[1] Lü Pu-
wei, we learn (I can only give the story in its barest
outlines) was a rich merchant of Wei, born near the
present K'ai-fêng Fu about 300 B.C., who had made
a fortune by 'buying things up when they were cheap
and selling them when they became dear.' Meeting
with an exiled prince of Ch'in he decided that 'here
indeed was a wonderful piece of goods to put in
stock.' The prince took a fancy to one of Lü Pu-wei's
concubines, a dancing-girl of Han-tan, who was preg-
nant. Presumably the father was Lü Pu-wei himself,
though this is not explicitly stated. Lü Pu-wei, pursuing his scheme of investment, presented the girl to
the prince and by wholesale bribery succeeded in
getting the prince acknowledged as Heir Apparent of
Ch'in. In 249 B.C. the prince succeeded to the throne,
but died three years later and was in turn succeeded
by the dancing-girl's son, now a boy of thirteen. The
new king being a minor, the whole power fell into
the hands of Lü Pu-wei, who continued to have intimate relations with the king's mother. At last in order
to escape from this entanglement, which as the king
grew older was becoming dangerous, Lü Pu-wei
adopted a singular stratagem. During a scene of
revelry he persuaded a certain Lao Ai, who was
famous for the great size of his yin, to parade the
gathering with his yin thrust through the centre of a
carriage wheel, and saw to it that the king's mother
heard of this scene. She at once determined (as Lü
Pu-wei had intended) to secure Lao Ai as her lover.
Lao Ai was then disguised as a eunuch, the head of

[1] Ch. 85.

the eunuchs being bribed to keep the secret, and was installed as personal attendant in the Dowager Queen's apartments. After a time the king, now grown to years of discretion, discovered the plot, executed Lao Ai and banished Lü Pu-wei who, after living for a time in constant dread of further punishment, ultimately drank poison.

The dancing-girl's child, now king of Ch'in, was no less a person than Shih Huang Ti, the First Emperor, founder of the Ch'in Empire and conqueror of all China. In short he was a hero, and even if we had not been told so, we might have guessed that, like most heroes, he was a bastard. We might also guess that, like so many heroes, he would kill his father; and in a sense this is what the story says he did, for it is told in such a way as to leave little doubt that Lü Pu-wei was the First Emperor's father and to suggest that the son drove the father to suicide. The life of Lü Pu-wei is in fact legend not history. But, as I have said, it illustrates the views that were popularly held about the power and wickedness of merchants.

At the opposite end of the pole to merchants, regarded by the Realist as harmful amoralists, came the harmful moralists, who preached virtues such as attachment to parents and loyalty to friends. These 'good people' maintain contact with and protect 'parents and friends who have disobeyed the law'; whereas 'bad' people disassociate themselves from them and denounce them. If the 'good' are given prominence, offences against the law will be concealed; if the 'bad' are given free play, crimes will be punished. When offences are concealed, the people become stronger than the Law; when crimes are punished, the Law is stronger than the people. When the people are stronger than the Law, there will be disorders in the land; when the Law is stronger than the people, the land will be powerful in war. Therefore it is said, 'one who has virtuous people to rule over will certainly suffer from upheavals and loss of territory; one who has bad people to rule over can secure order and military power.'[1]

The amoralism of *Shang Tzu* goes much further than that of *Han Fei Tzu*. Twice we are told that to do things that the enemy would be ashamed to do is the way to secure an advantage.[2]

To a special class of moralist that should be particularly discouraged belong the philanthropists who want to save the poor and starving by giving them land. But take the case of two men, otherwise on an equal footing. One of them, without the help of particularly good harvests or additional sources of income, manages to provide for himself adequately, simply by hard work and thrift. Another, without the disadvantage of bad harvests or of long illnesses or other disasters and troubles, falls into poverty and distress, simply owing to extravagance and idleness. The one becomes poor through extravagance and idleness, the other rich through hard work and thrift. If the ruler then taxes the rich in order to give to the poor, this simply means despoiling the industrious and thrifty in order to give to the extravagant and idle. To do this and at the same time expect the people to work hard and practise economy, is to demand the impossible.[3]

We have seen that all ways of thought other than Realism were to be suppressed. All book-learning is

[1] *Shang Tzu*, 5, pp. 38 and 39.
[2] 4, p. 28, and 20, p. 132.
[3] *Han Fei Tzu*, 50, p. 64.

dismissed as useless; even Realist treatises and hand-books on war and agriculture. 'Today everyone talks about methods of government and there is not a family that does not possess a copy of the laws of Shang Tzu and Kuan Tzu. But despite this the land grows poorer and poorer. Those who talk about agri-culture are many; those who hold the plough, few. Everyone talks about the art of warfare and there is not a family that does not possess a copy of *Sun Tzu* and *Wu Tzu*,[1] but our armies grow weaker and weaker. Those who talk about fighting are many; those who put on armour are few.'[2]

The Realists, as I have said, were concerned with 'actual facts' and condemned all reliance on super-natural guidance: 'that a State should use times and days, serve ghosts and spirits, trust in divination by the tortoise or by the yarrow-stalks, be addicted to prayers and sacrifices, is a portent of doom.'[3] Han Fei Tzu complains that the rulers of the day shower benefits upon 'diviners, palmists and sorcerers,' while the services of those who 'fight and conquer, attack and take' go unrewarded.[4] But the dividing line between superstition and science was hard to draw. In 213 B.C., eight years after the unification of China under the Ch'in dynasty, the general public were for-bidden to possess books other than those that were considered of practical utility; as useful, along with works on medicine and agriculture, were classed treatises on divination 'by the tortoise and by the yarrow-stalks.' Soothsayers are indeed a class that no society has ever wholly eliminated.

[1] Treatises on the art of war.
[2] *Han Fei Tzu*, 49, p. 59.
[3] *Han Fei Tzu*, 15, p. 1.
[4] 45, p. 31.

Last come the swashbucklers. Looked at from their own point of view they were fearless men who took upon themselves to protect the people from official oppression, to rescue from the clutches of the law those who had been wrongfully condemned, to 'take away from the rich in order to give to the poor.' Thus in their own view they were something like knight-errants. But whereas the medieval knight-errant was a single quixotic individual, accompanied at the most by one devoted squire, the Chinese *hsieh* ('protectors') roamed about in large bands. Ssu-ma Ch'ien, who has a chapter[1] about them, confesses that it was in practice often difficult to distinguish them from common brigands. To the Realist the *hsieh* who championed the oppressed and the *hsieh* who perhaps with noble motives picked pockets or broke into tombs were equally obnoxious. Both pitted 'private swords' against the public armoury of Law. Short-sighted princes found it convenient to employ these quixotic gangsters as *condottieri*; but not even a ruler 'mightier than ten Yellow Emperors put together' can maintain Law by means of forces that defy Law.

One of the tasks which the *hsieh* took upon themselves was the carrying out of vendetta on behalf of women and minors. According to the 'ways of Chou,' as defined by the Confucians, the task of punishing a murderer did not fall upon the State or the public at large. It was a duty incumbent upon the murdered man's sons, and in a lesser degree upon his brothers and friends.[2] 'If his father or mother has been slain, he must sleep on a bedding of straw with his buckler as pillow, he must hold no public office, but dedicate

[1] *Shih Chi*, 124.
[2] *Li Chi*, 1.

himself to vengeance so long as he and his enemy are under the same sky.'[1]

The existence of such a custom was obviously at variance with the Realist's principles. To him vendettas were 'private quarrels,' encroachments upon the sovereignty of Law, which alone holds the scales that mete out life and death. But the custom of vendetta was as deep-rooted in China as it is in many European countries today, and we find Chinese rulers several centuries later still vainly trying to suppress it.

The Past

Realism founds itself not merely 'on actual facts,' but on 'the facts of the world as it now exists.' The 'ways of the Former Kings,' diligently pieced together by the Confucians, cannot be those of the modern ruler confronted with modern problems. If, as the Confucians claim, Government by Goodness succeeded in the past, that was because 'men were few and things many.' Under such circumstances it is easy to be mild and accommodating. That the population must have increased is easy to prove. 'If a man has five children it is not considered a large family. Suppose each of these children in turn has five children, even during the life of the grandfather there are already twenty-five descendants.'[2] As the population grew, an age of *tê* (inner power) gave way to one of cunning, and this in turn was followed by the

[1] *Li Chi*, 111.
[2] *Han Fei Tzu*, 49, p. 53.

age of violence in which we now live. Any attempt to use in these days of violent competition the gentle methods of antiquity is doomed to complete failure.

That is why the Confucians, who continually criticize modern rulers for not adopting the ways of the past, are a danger to any State which tolerates them. But the habit of appealing to the past was deeply ingrained, and we find Realist writers slipping into it unawares. The very idea of a unified China was derived from legends about the past, and sometimes the ancient rulers, instead of being dismissed as humanitarians who solved by kindness the easy problems of a non-competitive age, are cited as successful exponents of Realism.

The Ruler

Almost the whole of Realist literature takes the form of advice to a ruler, or is concerned with the relations between the ruler and his ministers. It is assumed that the object of every ruler is to become a 'hegemon,' that is to say, to make his State paramount over all States or, at the best, to become ruler of all China. This can only be done if his State is stronger in war and richer than all the other States put together, and these ends can only be achieved if Law is substituted for morality and the whole energy of the State concentrated upon war and agriculture. Once the Realist State is created, the ruler will have little to do except amuse himself. But the creation of this State requires the observance by the ruler of certain secret methods and precautions, called his 'art' (shu).

For example, he must never reveal his own personal wishes or ideas. 'If he reveals his wishes, the ministers will carve and polish themselves' in conformity with these wishes, and he will not know their real nature. If he reveals his ideas, the ministers will 'turn their coats' in conformity with these ideas, and he will not discover their real opinion. He must confide in no one, not even in his own children; for if he confides, say, in one of his sons, the ministers will use the influence of this prince in order to further their own private interests.

The law cannot of course work merely mechanically; it requires men to operate it. But these men should so far as possible be mechanically chosen by Law itself. 'The enlightened ruler lets the Law choose men; he does not find them himself. He lets the Law weigh achievements; he does not measure them himself.'[1] That is to say, the law clearly defines what services entitle a man to be given a post and what achievements entitle him to promotion. Officials are not to be chosen because they have a good reputation or because they are learned, kind or eloquent. Nor, once they have been appointed, can the ruler keep watch over all their activities; 'the day is not long enough, nor one man's strength sufficient.' Moreover if they know that he has his eye upon them this will merely make them 'fake' the sort of conduct that they think he would like to witness; if he keeps his ears open, this will merely make them 'fake' the sort of sounds that they think he would like to hear. He sets out clearly his list of rewards and penalties, and lets the law take its course. 'Those who show capacity for their work and carry out what they have promised are rewarded; those who show incapacity

[1] *Han Fei Tzu*, 6, p. 23.

and do not carry out what they promised are punished.' And as is only logical 'those who promise little and perform much are also punished. Not that the ruler is not pleased at what they have done; but he knows that the harm of "words" not fitting "realities" is greater than the gain of even the highest achievement. That is why he punishes.'[1]

In a badly governed State the lower officials who desire promotion all say 'By heavy enough bribes one can get any high post that one wants,' and they say, 'For us to hope for promotion without first bribing our superiors is like baiting a mouse-trap with cat's flesh. It is quite useless. To hope for promotion owing to real work done for our superiors is like trying to get up a tall tree by holding on to a broken rope. It is even more useless than trying to do without bribery. As neither of these ways is any good, how can we be expected not to bleed those below us in order that we may be rich enough to bribe those above, and so obtain promotion?'[2]

The ruler must therefore see to it that promotion is obtained by services rigorously defined by law, and be on his guard against corruption and bribery. There are eight means by which bad ministers scheme against a ruler. They may make presents of gold and jade to his bed-fellows—to his wife or maybe to some boy favourite or concubine who will take advantage of him when he is disporting himself at his ease and has eaten and drunk heavily, wheedling him into making promises that are against his better judgment. Or they may bribe his jesters and dwarfs who, being always at his side, have ample opportunity of studying his moods and fancies, to throw in a

[1] Han Fei Tzu, 7, p. 27.
[2] Shang Tzu, 3, p. 20.

casual word which may induce him to countenance some illegal practice.

Those to whom a ruler naturally turns for advice are his elder relatives on the one hand and his chief minister and Court officials on the other. Bad ministers will attempt to suborn the former by entertaining them with music and handsome pages and women; the latter, by promises of promotion and increase of salary.

Again, ministers know well enough that rulers delight in fine palaces, in towers and ornamental lakes, in fine clothes for their women and pages and handsome trappings for their horses and dogs. By procuring these things for the ruler they distract his attention from public business and are able to further their own private needs unimpeded. Another device is to curry favour with the mob by petty acts of kindness which increase their own popularity and make the ruler seem harsh in comparison. Then again they may send for clever speakers from other countries and patronize insinuating talkers of their own land who will instil into the ruler's mind whatever false impressions these schemers wish to inspire.

And lastly, there are more violent methods. They may collect about them armed desperadoes and terrorize the Court, or intrigue with powerful neighbouring countries who will with their connivance mass threatening armies on the frontier and leave the ruler no choice but to yield.[1]

A ruler must never forget that there are those near him who desire his death. 'A man of fifty is still capable of falling in love; but a woman of thirty has already lost her charm. A wife who has lost her charm, married to a husband who still falls in love,

[1] *Han Fei Tzu,* 9.

is bound to anticipate a time when she will be out of favour, in which case her son will no longer be regarded as Heir Apparent. That is why queens and consorts often desire the death of their lord.'[1] Such are some of the dangers to which a ruler is exposed. But if he is equipped with the true arts (*shu*) of kingship, then he may cheerfully spend his time 'netting and fowling, coursing and chasing, beating his bells and setting his maidens to dance. His country will be none the worse.'[2]

Power

Shên Tao,[3] a Taoist who lived about 300 B.C., developed a special theory about the art of ruling. According to him the mere fact that a king is a king—what Shên Tao calls his position (*shih*) as king—endows him with power (*shih*); he needs no other qualities or capacities. Like many mystical doctrines, this belief is based upon a pun. The two words *shih* ('potency,' 'power,' 'force') and *shih* ('position,' 'circumstance,' 'situation') were not merely identical in sound but happen to be written with the same character. It was natural therefore that they should be regarded as having some mysterious connection. On the same principle Mr. Lansbury once said, 'I am proud of being called a crank; after all, the crank is a very important part in many machines.'

Power (*shih*) thus comes to the monarch auto-

[1] *Han Fei Tzu*, 17, p. 6.
[2] *Han Fei Tzu*, 44, p. 28.
[3] See Appendix II.

matically owing to his situation (*shih*), and he has only to avail himself of it, as the dragon rides the storm-cloud, and there will be order in the land. He need not in himself be either wiser or better than other men.

The Realists did not in general use the word 'power' in this punning, mystic sense, in which indeed it is almost equivalent to the older word *tê* ('inborn power') as used by Chuang Tzu and Lao Tzu. They meant by it not some mysterious potency that 'is so of itself'—that is 'natural,' as we should say—but simply the power that human beings can come by, nothing more,[1] the power that accrues to those who can harm people or frighten them, and who are not ashamed to do so.

In a very closely reasoned passage Han Fei Tzu explains his own attitude towards the controversy that Shên Tao's theory had aroused. The critics of Shên Tao argued that if all kings have this mysterious quality in virtue of the mere fact that they are kings, and if the possession of it ensures good rule, bad rule would never occur. How then are we to account for the tyrants Chieh and Chou? The defenders of Shên Tao replied that bad kings did indeed possess 'power,' but used it to produce disorder instead of order. Han Fei Tzu, in his turn, shows that both disputants are using the term 'power' in the sense 'power automatically derived from the mere fact of being king'; whereas when the Realists say (just as Shên Tao did) that the ruler needs no moral qualities or special capacities, they mean that he rules solely by 'acquired power,' by the forces that enable him to hold men's lives in the balance. They are not supporting a mystical theory of 'natural power.' The

[1] *Han Fei Tzu*, 40, p. 16.

whole passage[1] shows in an interesting manner how the Realists tended to borrow Taoist maxims, but apply them in a way of their own.

The Art of the Courtier

The greater part of Realist literature is, as I have said, concerned with the art of ruling. An exception is the twelfth chapter of Han Fei Tzu, which is an essay on how the courtier should deal with the king. Because the advice that it contains is irreconcilable with the advice given to monarchs in other chapters, the authenticity of this essay has been doubted. I do not see why it should be assumed that Han Fei Tzu was incapable of inconsistency; but the point is not worth arguing, for we are here concerned with thought rather than with literary history, and it is fortunately not our business to discover whether this or any other chapter of Han Fei Tzu is actually the work of the master.

Han Fei is said to have stammered; but he protests that he has in reality no impediment of speech. 'Your servant Fei,' he says in a memorial[2] to the Ch'in king, 'is not hard of speech. The reason that he finds it hard to speak is that one who speaks fluently, smoothly, with eloquence and grace of diction, is regarded as showy but unsound; a speech that is respectful and sober, firm, careful and thorough, is regarded as clumsy and ill-composed. A speech that is copious and fully supported by instances, analogies

[1] 40, pp. 14-16.
[2] Han Fei Tzu, 3.

and comparisons is regarded as empty and impracticable; one that sums up the essentials in a few words, is direct, brief and unadorned, is regarded as curt and ineloquent. A speech that touches too pointedly upon the personal and near and shows deep understanding of another's feelings is regarded as presumptuous and intrusive; one that is general and wide, subtle, remote and deep is regarded as pretentious and unpractical. He who uses homely counsels and fables to enforce his points is regarded as unrefined.

'He whose words suit the age and whose opinions are not at variance with his master's is regarded as a flatterer, anxious only to save his own skin; words that are far removed from what is customary and are startling to ordinary men are regarded as mere ravings. He who speaks with lively address and copious eloquence, abounding in literary adornments, is called a clerk; he who discards learning and literature and speaks solidly and naturally is called uncultivated. He who on occasion cites the *Songs* or *Book of History* and in his doctrines bases himself upon the past is considered a text-droner. That is why your servant Fei finds difficulty in speaking and is heavily grieved.'

I will now translate the famous twelfth chapter, omitting only a phrase or two where the text is corrupt, and some anecdotes of a not very interesting character by means of which the author illustrates his arguments. The whole chapter is reproduced in the biography of Han Fei Tzu,[1] and I have used both texts.

If it is admittedly a difficult thing to address a ruler this is not so much due to the difficulty of understand-

[1] *Shih Chi*, 63. Han Fei Tzu was a member of the ruling family of the State of Han, which lay on the eastern

ing the matter in hand and knowing what ought to be said, nor to the difficulty of finding words with which to give eloquent expression to one's ideas. . . . The difficulty of addressing a ruler consists in the difficulty of understanding his state of mind and knowing how to adapt one's arguments to it.

Suppose, for example, the monarch you are addressing is bent on maintaining a high reputation and you appeal to him only on grounds of material gain, he will regard you as a person of low principles, treat you with no consideration or respect and henceforward exclude you from his confidence. If, on the other hand, he is bent on material gain and you appeal to him on grounds of reputation, he will regard you as lacking in common sense and out of contact with realities, and will not make use of you. Again, if he is secretly bent on material gain but professes outwardly to care only for maintaining a high reputation, should you appeal to him on grounds of reputation, he will pretend to be pleased with you, but in reality will keep you at a distance; should you appeal to him on grounds of material gain, he will secretly follow your advice, but will outwardly disown you. All this must be taken into consideration.

Success in public business depends on secrecy; the leakage of a few words may mean ruin. It may happen, without any actual leakage, that something you say sounds like an allusion to a secret policy of the person you are addressing. In such a case, your life may be in danger. Sometimes his declared motive will be quite different from what he really has in view. If you show him that you understand not only his avowed motive

---

fronticrs of Ch'in. His works were addressed chiefly to the king of Han. In 233 B.C. he was sent on a mission to Ch'in, where he attempted to persuade the king of Ch'in not to annex Han. His mission was unsuccessful; he was detained in Ch'in and committed suicide, the poison (it is said) being courteously provided by the Ch'in minister, Li Ssu.

but also his real object, your life will be in danger. If some clever person[1] is successful in inferring from what has happened in other cases the course that the ruler has told you he intends to pursue and the secret leaks out, you will certainly be supposed to have let it out and your life will be in danger.

Do not waste your whole wisdom upon him before you have fully insinuated yourself into his confidence. If he follows your advice and is successful, you will get no credit for it; if he neglects your advice and comes to grief, he will suspect you,[2] and your life will be in danger. Never quote rules of ritual and of etiquette to a high personage who has made a mistake, in order to prove to him that he is in the wrong. If you do so, your life will be in danger. If a high personage puts into force a policy that is successful and wants to take the whole credit for it, do not remind him that you too were in favour of it, or your life will be in danger. Do not try to force him to do what he lacks the power to do, or stop him from doing what he is incapable of giving up; if you do so, your life will be in danger.

If you talk to him favourably about his higher ministers, he will think you intend a reproach to himself; if you talk favourably about persons of less importance, he will think you are selling your influence. If you speak of those he is fond of, he will think you are making free with his property; if you speak of those he dislikes, he will think you are doing it to see what he will say. If you speak shortly and to the point, he will think you are too stupid to say more; if you flood him with a stream of learning and eloquence, he will think you importunate and pedantic. If you give only a cursory expression to your ideas, he will say you are too timid to come to the point; if you go into everything, fully

[1] Text a little uncertain; but general sense clear.
[2] Of having given him away to his enemies in order to justify yourself.

and frankly, he will say you are ill-bred and presumptuous.

Such are the difficulties of addressing a ruler, and it is indispensable that they should be properly understood.

The speaker should spare no pains to discover how best to bring into prominence the things that the person he is addressing is proud of and to cover up what he is ashamed of. For example, if he is in private difficulties, set forth the matter and bring pressure to bear upon him entirely from the standpoint of public duty. If he is apt to be discouraged by his own evil propensities but is unable to master them, the speaker should lay stress upon his finer qualities and gloss over his failures. If he is apt to be self-satisfied, but does not live up to his conception of himself, the speaker should call attention to his mistakes, and make him aware of his bad qualities and lay stress on his failure to live up to his principles.

If the person you are addressing prides himself upon his cleverness, then give him scope by citing cases that though different belong to the same class as the matter under discussion. In this way you can make him take his topics from you, pretending to be ignorant yourself in order to give him a chance to show his cleverness. If you wish him to adopt a course that you know will be in every way advantageous to him, then advocate it upon the ground that it will enhance his public reputation, only hinting in a faint way that his private interests will be served. If on the other hand you wish him to abandon a project that you regard as dangerous, then assert openly that his reputation will suffer, hinting only in a faint way that his private interests will suffer.

If you praise other persons whose conduct was like that of the ruler you are addressing or cite instances of the same policy having been pursued in dealing with other cases, then if the vices of these other persons were the same as those of the ruler whom you are addressing, you must be sure to make it appear that such vices are innocuous, and if the policy you are advocating failed in other cases (?) you must be sure to make it clear that no great harm ensued.

If he prides himself on his power, do not twit him with the things he is not strong enough to do; if he prides himself on quickness of decision, do not provoke him by mentioning his hesitations;[1] if he prides himself on the wisdom of his policies, do not relentlessly bring home to him his failures.

If in your general purport there is nothing to offend him and in your choice of words nothing to affront him, you may confidently proceed to deploy all the wisdom and eloquence of which you dispose. Such is the proper way to obtain intimacy and confidence and be in a position to speak your mind to the full . . .

Then as time goes quietly on and you become more and more firmly established in the prince's favour, you may embark upon deeper plans without losing his confidence and criticize or oppose him without incurring punishment, till by openly advocating what will be advantageous to him and condemning what will be harmful you promote his achievements, and by bluntly pointing out what will be considered right and what wrong you embellish his reputation; so that both you and he fulfil your tasks. At this point the art of addressing a ruler reaches its perfection . . .

The dragon is a creature which is docile and can be tamed and ridden. But under its neck are reversed scales which stick out a full foot, and anyone who comes in contact with them loses his life. A ruler of men is much like the dragon; he too has reversed scales, and an adviser who knows how to keep clear of them will not go far wrong.

[1] Text uncertain.

Epilogue

Of the three ways of thought described in this book only one was ever officially adopted and put into practice. There was never a Taoist State as conceived by Chuang Tzu, nor a Confucian State as conceived by Mencius. Government by Goodness had been tried, people said, by the legendary king Yen of Hsü once upon a time, no one quite knew when; but by goodness 'king Yen lost his kingdom and destroyed the land of Hsü.' Realism, on the other hand, was not merely adopted by the ruler of a great State, but on being put into action was found to do everything that was expected of it. An excellent account of the triumph of Realism has been given by Dr. Derk Bodde in his *China's First Unifier*. Political history is not the main subject of my present book, and I will here give only a brief sketch of the steps by which the western land of Ch'in gradually got the whole of China into its power.

In 247 B.C. Ch'in took into its service a man of Ch'u called Li Ssu, who like Han Fei Tzu was a pupil of the Confucian philosopher Hsün Tzu. Like Han Fei Tzu, again, Li Ssu soon turned from Confucianism to Realism. From about 235 onwards he became more and more influential in Ch'in. His policy was the complete conquest of China. He insisted that such an adventure was practicable. 'Ours,' he said, 'is such a chance as does not come once in ten thousand years.' In 230 Ch'in annexed Han; in

228, Chao; in 225, Wei; in 223, Ch'u; in 222, Yen; and finally in 221 Ch'i, the last State to maintain its independence, surrendered to Ch'in, and the whole of China was united under the rule of the king of Ch'in, who became 'Shih Huang-ti,' First Emperor.

In 213 Li Ssu introduced a measure which forbade the public to possess any literature save technical handbooks.[1] In 212 hundreds of scholars were executed or exiled, on the charge that they had criticized the régime. In 210 the First Emperor died while on a journey, and in 206 the Ch'in dynasty collapsed, having ruled China for fifteen years.

For an account of the way in which Realist ideas were put into practice I must refer the reader to special studies of the period.[2] But one question arises which concerns us more immediately. The writings of the Realists were addressed to the monarch and occasionally to his ministers, but never to the general public. When the Realist State communicated with the public, when it undertook what we call propaganda, did it dare to present its doctrines in their nakedness, or had it one ethic for official guidance and quite another for public consumption?

A clear answer is found in the inscriptions put up in various places in China that were visited by the Emperor. Nominally they were the work of admiring officials who asked to be allowed to celebrate the Emperor's virtues; we may in any case be sure that they represent what the Emperor and his advisers wanted to be generally believed. Now in these inscriptions the spectre of Realism is assiduously muffled in the trappings of traditional morality. The

[1] See above, p. 174.
[2] Particularly, Dr. Bodde's work, referred to above, and J. J. L. Duyvendak's The Book of Lord Shang.

Ch'ins are not represented as having embarked upon the subjugation of China because they had a chance of conquest such as 'does not come once in ten thousand years,' but because all the other rulers were wicked tyrants who were maltreating their people. The Realists mocked in private at traditional rites; an inscription of 219 B.C. boasts that everyone under this happy régime conforms to the rites. The Realists despised 'goodness and morality'; another inscription of 219 exalts them. Other inscriptions claim that wives have become more chaste, husbands less adulterous; in fact there has been, as the inscription of 210 says, a 'cleaning up of manners.'

All this sounds more like Confucianism than Realism, and it is not surprising to find that one of the earlier inscriptions was actually made 'in consultation with the Confucian teachers of Lu.' On the other hand, the main emphasis in the inscriptions is on the administrative measures of the Ch'in conquerors— the codification of law, the unification of script and of weights and measures, the abolition of feudal domains and division of the whole Empire into administrative districts. These inscriptions set the tone of official propaganda for two thousand years. It was in much the same terms that the Manchu emperors still continued to address their subjects well into the twentieth century. The fall of the Ch'ins was not immediately followed by a reaction in favour of Right as opposed to Might, of morality as opposed to universal State-imposed Law. It was not until after the middle of the 2nd century B.C., some seventy years after the rise of the Hans, that Confucianism began to receive official encouragement. Till then there prevailed the same curious blend of Taoist mysticism and Realist amoralism that had inspired the previous régime.

The Taoists held that the object of life should be the cultivation of inner powers; the Confucians, that it should be the pursuit of Goodness. The Realists for the most part ignored the individual, and though there are passages that envisage an ultimate peaceful utopia, their general assumption is that the object of any society is to dominate other societies. These views are none of them idiosyncracies peculiar to ancient China. The first is still widely held in India and by those elsewhere who have been influenced by Indian thought. The second is the view of religious teachers in America and most parts of Europe. The third is held by a number of vigorous and expanding States. All these views are therefore of immediate interest to us, and that is why I have made them the main subject of this book. But the period with which I have dealt was marked by an unparalleled fecundity of ideas; it is indeed known as the time of the Hundred Schools, though the 'hundred' is of course not to be taken as more than a convenient round number. I have made little mention of various schools about which a good deal could be said. For example, the dialecticians only appear incidentally; their works are too technical to be of interest to the general public, and have survived in so corrupt a form that they can only be discussed in connection with highly specialized problems of text criticism and philology. The Cosmologists, who believed in a mysterious parallel between the structure of man and the universe, I have not mentioned at all.[1] Their

[1] For an example of the application of their ideas to imaginary ritual, see Appendix IV.

theories (for example, the equation of colours with points of the compass) perhaps go back to something fundamental, for similar ideas crop up, to all appearances quite independently, in parts of North America and Africa. But in their detailed working out such theories become too mechanical and arbitrary to be of compelling interest.

Some readers may feel that since ideas do not drop ready-made from the sky but are determined (as I would readily admit) by the environment of the thinkers, I ought to have said more about the nature of the society in which these three ways of thought flourished. The ancient Chinese, they will say, were agriculturalists, but not dairymen, drove horses but did not ride them,[1] used oxen to draw carts but not for ploughing,[2] were strongly patrilineal with a tendency to foster the clan and family at the expense of larger groups, were ancestor-worshippers whose whole economy was bound up with the need for obtaining exotic substances used in the cult of the dead; had 'divine kings' who controlled the weather and the crops and a social system which postulated a rigid division between 'gentlemen' and 'common people,' and so on. Cannot you tell us how the philosophies that you describe fit into this environment?

If I make no attempt to do so, it is because I believe in division of labour. To deal adequately with the history of thought requires a special training and a suitable temperament. Too many of the existing books about Chinese thought have been the work of writers who reacted as feebly to the thoughts of Mencius and Chuang Tzu as a Hottentot would react to the news that Blue Peter had won the

[1] Till about 300 B.C.
[2] Till about 200 B.C.

Derby. The task of analysing Chinese institutions, for example, methods of trade, land-tenure, taxation, legal procedure, demands in its turn quite another training and a different temperament. Moreover, the gaps in our knowledge are immense. Even as late as the 3rd century B.C. China was still divided into at least six independent States. No serious study has as yet been made as to the ways in which the cultures of these States differed from one another. We know hardly anything about foreign trade, nor do we know when iron was introduced nor what was its quality; we do not know, as far as I can see, even when the cultivation of wet rice came to China.

That is why, being myself a student of thought and literature rather than of institutions or history, I have confined myself in the main to an account of ideas, regarding it as someone else's job to discover how ways of thought were linked to ways of living.

Appendices

THE SOURCES

(1) *Chuang Tzu*

There are several complete translations; in reality they are often translations of the commentaries rather than of the text. Unfortunately the text itself is so corrupt as to be frequently quite unintelligible. I have used only such passages as are completely intelligible or which need merely trivial and occasional correction. Scholarly study of the text only began in the 18th century. Important work was done by a long line of scholars culminating in the quite recent 'Modern Commentary' (*Chin Chien*) of Kao Hêng and the brilliant 'supplementary commentary' to the first seven chapters by Chu Kuei-yao. For variants and parallel passages the *Chuang Tzu I Chêng* of Ma Hsü-lun is invaluable; but his emendations are wild.

Theories about which chapters are 'genuine' have little real meaning. *Chuang Tzu* does not purport to be a work by Chuang Tzu, but merely contains a certain number of anecdotes about him. Some parts are by a splendid poet, others are by a feeble scribbler; but there is no evidence that the good parts are earlier than the bad ones. The only chapter that is almost certainly an irrelevant addition is the thirtieth, the Discourse on Swords. This lacks the commentary of Kuo Hsiang (died A.D. 312), and was probably added between the 4th and the 7th century by someone who wrongly identified the Chuang Tzu of this story with Chuang Tzu the Taoist.

(2) Lieh Tzu

I have used several passages from Lieh Tzu, a Taoist collection which overlaps with Chuang Tzu, containing eighteen identical or almost identical passages. There is also one passage[1] that we know to have occurred in a version of Chuang Tzu considerably longer than the existing one, which was commented upon by Ssu-ma Piao, who died in A.D. 328. It is probable that a good many other passages in Lieh Tzu also occurred in the longer version of Chuang Tzu. Indeed, the early date of more than half of Lieh Tzu is guaranteed by the fact that identical or almost identical passages occur in works of the 3rd century B.C. or in books such as Huai-nan Tzu (2nd century B.C.) which consist chiefly of extracts from earlier books.

I mention these facts because it is currently held in China that Lieh Tzu is of much later date than Chuang Tzu. Thus Fung Yu-lan in his History of Chinese Philosophy (Chinese edition, p. 619; not yet translated) says that Lieh Tzu is a work of the 3rd or 4th century A.D. He and others have said that the Hedonist chapter (the seventh) of Lieh Tzu is in-

[1] The young man and the sea-gulls, Lieh Tzu, II, j.

consistent with the ideas of the 3rd century B.C. But the hedonistic doctrine which the wicked brothers expound to Tzu-ch'an in *Lieh Tzu* is identical with that which the wicked brother Chih expounds to Confucius in *Chuang Tzu*. According to Fung Yu-lan's argument the Robber Chih chapter in *Chuang Tzu* must also belong to the 3rd or 4th century A.D.; but although this chapter has always shocked Confucians, neither he nor so far as I know anyone else has ever suggested that it is a work of the 3rd century A.D.

In several cases where *Lieh Tzu* has passages which also occur in books later than the 3rd century B.C. there is no evidence which way round the borrowing is; sometimes *Lieh Tzu* and the later text may both have been using a common source. In certain passages of *Lieh Tzu* critics have seen references to Buddhism; thus the anecdote (VIII, 24) about 'releasing living things' as part of a New Year ceremony has been interpreted as referring to the Buddhist custom of *fang-shêng* ('release of live things'). It remains to be proved that this Buddhist custom was known in China at anything like so early a date as the 3rd or 4th century A.D., the period to which critics attribute the forging of *Lieh Tzu*.

The quotation from the *Mu T'ien Tzu Chuan* (rediscovered in A.D. 281) which follows the story of king Mu and the wizard (*Lieh Tzu*, ch. 3)[1] is an obvious interpolation. The wizard has just explained that the king's journeyings were not actual travels in a geographical sense, but 'wanderings of the soul.' Legend, however, attributed to king Mu an actual westward journey, and some unreflecting copyist has inserted an account of this physical journey, not see-

[1] See above, p. 40.

ing that by doing so he destroyed the whole intention of *Lieh Tzu's* fable.

(3) *Mencius*

I have written and hope to publish elsewhere a discussion of the textual difficulties in Mencius. Here I have chosen passages where few such difficulties occur. Chiao Hsün's edition (A.D. 1819) reprinted in the Basic Sinological series is the best at present available.

(4) *Han Fei Tzu*

I have used the Wang Hsien-shên edition in the Basic Sinological series.

(5) *Shang Tzu*

This text has been translated and amply commented upon by Professor Duyvendak in his *The Book of Lord Shang* (Probsthain, 1928). I have used the edition of Ch'ên Ch'i-t'ien, published by the Shanghai Commercial Press (1935).

(6) *Mo Tzu*

I have used Sun I-jang's *Mo Tzu Hsien Ku* (1909).

(7) *Hsün Tzu*

Liang Ch'i-hsiung's *Hsün Tzu Chien Shih* (1936).

HSÜN TZU ON MENCIUS

'There are some who in a fragmentary way take the Former Kings as their model, but fail to understand them as a whole. Nevertheless they show considerable ability and strength of purpose, their knowledge is varied and wide. They preach a doctrine for which they claim great antiquity—the so-called theory of the Five Elements. It is extremely peculiar and inconsistent. It is full of mysteries and enigmas which are not solved, of secrets and short cuts that are never explained. In order to give colour to their statements and win respect for them, these people say: "That is what was taught by true gentlemen in former times; Tzu Ssu sang this tune and Mencius took up the song."

'The ordinary, low, unintelligent Confucian of the present day accordingly welcomes such teaching with delight, quite unable to see that there is anything wrong with it. And having received it, he hands it on to his pupils, imagining that it was because of doctrines such as these that Confucius and his disciples were valued by the generations that succeeded them.

'Such people have done a grave injustice[1] to Tzu Ssu and Mencius!' (*Hsün Tzu*, VI).

If my interpretation is right, the passage is not (as has been supposed) an attack on Mencius, but on the Cosmologists.

CHUANG TZU ON SHÊN TAO

'Shên Tao, discarding knowledge and the cultivation of self, merely followed the line of least resistance. He made an absolute indifference to outside things his sole way and principle. He said, "Wisdom consists in not knowing; he who thinks that by widening his knowledge he is getting nearer to wisdom is merely destroying wisdom."

'His views were so warped and peculiar that it was impossible to make use of him; yet he laughed at the world for honouring men of capacity. He was so lax and uncontrolled that one may say he had no principles at all; yet he railed at the world for making much of the Sages. He let himself be pounded and battered, scraped and broken, be rolled like a ball wherever things carried him. He had no use for "Is" and "Is not," but was bent only on getting through somehow. He did not school himself by knowledge or thought, had no understanding of what should come first and what last, but remained in utter indifference. Wherever he was pushed he went, wherever he was dragged he came, unstable as a feather that whirls at every passing breath of the wind, or a polished stone that slides at a mere touch.

[1] Cf. *Mencius*, VI, 2, VII. 'The Five Hegemons are sinners (*tsui jen*) against the Three Kings.'

'Yet he remained whole; nothing went amiss with him. Whether he moved or stood still, nothing went wrong, and never at any time did he give offence. What was the reason of this? I will tell you. Inanimate objects never make trouble for themselves. They do not burden themselves with knowledge, and yet never whether in motion or at rest do they depart from what is reasonable, and for this reason they never go wrong. That is what he meant by saying "all that is necessary is to make yourself like an inanimate object; do not try to be better or wiser than other people. A clod of earth cannot lose its way."

'The great men of the day used to laugh at him, saying that Shên Tao's principles were better suited to the dead than to the living, and might astonish, but certainly could not convince' (Chuang Tzu, XXXIII).

I give this passage because existing translations of it seem to me very imperfect.

(Mo Tzu, Ch. 68)

'When an enemy comes from the East, build an altar towards the East, eight feet high, and a hall with eight sides. Let eight men eighty years old preside over the offerings. They hold a blue banner with the Blue God (shên) painted upon it, and eight men eight feet tall with eight bows shoot eight arrows and no more. The general of the troops, dressed in blue, is then to sacrifice a cock.'

It would be tedious to go through all four points of the compass in full. For the south, the number is seven, the colour red and the sacrifice a dog; for the west, the equivalences are nine, white, and a goat; for the north, six, black, and a pig. 'The shapes of cloud-vapours are to be observed. There are those that stand for a commander-in-chief, for a lesser general, for coming and going, for victory and defeat. By understanding these, one may know whether the issue will be favourable or unfavourable.'

All the shamans (wu), medicine men and sooth-sayers are to have their appointed places, where they are to preside over the preparation of herbs. A good house is to be chosen for their quarters. The shamans must be near the public shrine. . . . 'The shamans and soothsayers tell the truth to the commander of the defences,[1] and he alone is to know the true facts, as reported by the shamans, soothsayers and inspectors of cloud-vapours. Those who go in and out spreading rumours and creating panic among the officials and people must be tracked down and ruthlessly punished.'

[1] Whereas the people must always be 'told that the omens are good. See Mo Tzu, 70.

APPENDIX IV

BIOGRAPHIES

(1) Of Chuang Tzu nothing is known (beyond what the book *Chuang Tzu* tells us in anecdotes which make no pretence to be historical) save that the *Shih Chi*[1] speaks of his having once been a minor official at Ch'i-yüan, a place in south-east Honan.

(2) Of Mencius (round whose name many legends gathered in later times) the *Shih Chi* can again tell us nothing that cannot be gathered from the book *Mencius*, except that he studied under a pupil of Confucius's grandson Tzu Ssu.

(3) The life of Han Fei Tzu consists almost entirely of extracts from his works. The story of his mission to Ch'in and suicide there reads like an extremely telescoped account of what was probably a much more complicated series of events.

(4) *Shang Tzu* is simply a cover-name; it would be irrelevant in this connection to give a biography of the historical Shang Tzu (died 338 B.C.). Concerning the author or authors of the book *Shang Tzu* nothing is known.

[1] Ch. 63.

Index